导游服务能力
——广东导游现场考试实务

广东省全国导游资格考试专家编写组 编

廣東旅游出版社
GUANGDONG TRAVEL & TOURISM PRESS
悦读书·悦旅行·悦享人生

中国·广州

图书在版编目（CIP）数据

导游服务能力：广东导游现场考试实务 / 广东省全国导游资格考试专家编
写组编 . -- 广州：广东旅游出版社，2024. 9. -- ISBN 978-7-5570-3383-5

Ⅰ . F590.63

中国国家版本馆 CIP 数据核字第 2024DK8856 号

出版人：刘志松

策划编辑：官　顺

责任编辑：林保翠　陈伊甜

装帧设计：谭敏仪

责任校对：李瑞苑

责任技编：冼志良

导游服务能力：广东导游现场考试实务

Daoyou Fuwu Nengli：Guangdong Daoyou Xianchang Kaoshi Shiwu

出版发行：广东旅游出版社

（广州市荔湾区沙面北街71号首、二层）

邮　　编：510130

电　　话：020-87347732（总编室）　020-87348887（销售热线）

投稿邮箱：2026542779@qq.com

印　　刷：佛山家联印刷有限公司

（佛山市南海区桂城街道三山新城科能路10号自编4号楼三层之一）

开　　本：787毫米×1092毫米　16开

印　　张：9

字　　数：208千字

版　　次：2024年9月第1版

印　　次：2024年9月第1次

定　　价：38.00元

本书编辑委员会

主　编

胡依明　　刘志松

副主编

李　静　　龚晓辉

编　委

（按姓氏笔画排序）

石超凡　　杨运举　　黄晓玲　　黄碧雅　　崔康晋　　瞿朝辉

英文编译

王晶晶　　罗　瑜

英文审读

陈　胜　　余　东　　高　巍

编写说明

2023年起，中国旅游业经历了显著的复苏和增长，文化和旅游部发布的《国内旅游提升计划（2023—2025年）》进一步释放了旅游消费潜力，使旅游业持续升温，呈现出强劲的发展态势。与此同时，旅游市场的多元化、个性化、深度化趋势明显，也为传统的旅游服务模式带来了新的挑战。

广东作为接待游客数量和旅游收入长期处于全国第一梯队的省份，旅游资源丰富多样，不但自然景观和历史遗迹兼有，主题公园、现代娱乐设施和城市旅游方面更是位处全国前列，打造了众多高质量、高知名度的旅游产品。广东也是"72/144小时过境免签政策"的实施省份，有3个入境口岸城市。广东的旅游业态也在不断变化、发展中，给导游队伍建设提出了更新、更高的要求。

为了响应国家对加快建设旅游强国，推动旅游业高质量发展的要求，我社组织了文化和旅游领域的企业精英、金牌资深导游和专业教师组成编写委员会，编撰了《导游服务能力——广东导游现场考试实务》一书，旨在为考生和从业者提供专业、精准的讲解知识和技巧，并实现"从试到岗"的顺利过渡。

本书的特点包括：

一、严格按照文化和旅游部相关文件精神和全国导游资格考试大纲要求编写。

二、详细说明和分析了考试流程及注意事项，附有机考系统的操作指南，让考生熟知流程，充分准备。同时，注意事项的仪容仪表和讲解要求等建议，亦是导游人员从业后的职场要求，常看熟记，有助于提升自身职业素养。

三、每个景区皆包含讲解要点、记忆技巧和思维导图，梳理脉络，逻辑归纳；讲解词提取关键词置于段前，让考生轻松把握讲解思路。

四、每个景区皆提供中英文讲解词示范，中文内容凸显文旅结合，英文内容则契合外国人的语言习惯和兴趣所在，既是考试讲解范本，亦可用于真实环境中的导游讲解。

五、彩色文字和波浪线突出显示，圈定重要信息和得分点。

六、思维导图全面、系统地展示完整信息，通过图像、颜色和线条等元素，增强记忆效果。

七、每个景区皆附有综合知识，从广度、深度扩展导游对该景区的知识储备。需要说明的是，讲解词示范都略超出考试讲解时间所应容纳的字数，这是因为考虑到考生语速、讲解风格和记忆力的差别，不宜逐句背诵，但可以根据自身特点记诵范文，也可以在综合知识板块选择更多知识点进行讲解词的写作，以更好地进行讲解准备。同时，为了避免大篇文字让考生记忆疲倦，综合知识采用罗列知识点的形式，更便于记忆和整合。这些综合知识对于已考取导游资格证的从业人员来说，也有一定的实用性。

本书由胡依明、刘志松担任主编。广州市旅游商务职业学校旅游专业资深教师、国家高级导游、首批广州金牌导游李静，国家高级导游、广东中旅导游培训师，广州市导游协会理事龚晓辉担任副主编。其中，李静负责第一章、第二章及第三章第1、11、13、15节的编撰和审校，龚晓辉负责第三章第2—10、12、14节的编撰和审校。

本书英文讲解词由广东省普通高校人文社科重点研究基地广东外语外贸大学南国商学院"多语种中华文化译介研究中心"团队编译和审校。其中，王晶晶、罗瑜负责英文编译，陈胜、余东、高巍负责英文审校。

中国旅游业蓬勃发展，日新月异，对导游人才的职业素质要求也在不断变化，本书在编写过程中，限于篇幅和时效，难免有所疏漏，但如能为中国旅游事业的广厦添砖加瓦，亦是我们从业者和出版者的幸事。本书将应旅游业态的发展和旅游人才的需求变化而持续修订，敬请社会行业专家批评指正。

广东旅游出版社

目录
CONTENTS

第一章
导游服务能力考试内容

第一节　广东导游服务能力考试大纲

《导游服务能力》考试大纲
（广东省）

一、考试目的

本科目考试（现场考试）是导游资格考试的重要组成部分，主要考查考生对广东主要景点的讲解能力和相关知识的掌握程度，以及对时政、经济、文化、入境便利化等综合知识的了解程度；考查考生对导游服务规范及工作程序的掌握和应用；考查考生处理突发事件和特殊问题的能力；考查外语考生在导游讲解过程中的现场翻译能力、口语水平。

二、考试内容

（一）景点讲解

主要是考查考生的导游讲解是否符合规范程序，考生对旅游景点的熟悉程度，以及讲解景点的语言能力，包括讲解内容的正确性、全面性、条理性，是否详略得当、重点突出，具有一定的讲解技巧，以及回答景点问题的正确性。考生先讲解景点，再回答三个与其余景点相关的问题。

1.中文类考试景点讲解范围：广州市长隆旅游度假区（概述及长隆野生动物世界）、广州市农民运动讲习所旧址（概述及崇圣殿）、深圳市华侨城旅游度假区（概述及锦绣中华民俗村）、珠海市海泉湾度假区（概述及海洋温泉）、佛山市西樵山景区（概述及白云洞景区）、韶关市丹霞山景区（概述及长老峰）、梅州市叶剑英纪念园（概述及叶剑英纪念馆）、中山市孙中山故里旅游区（概述及孙中山故居）、江门市开平碉楼与村落（自力村碉楼群）、阳江市广东海上丝绸之路博物馆景区（概述及"南海Ⅰ号"主题展区）、肇庆市七星岩风景区（概述及龙岩洞和摩崖石刻群）、潮州市广济桥文物旅游景区（概述及桥墩）。

2.外语类考试景点讲解范围：世界地质公园——丹霞山、开平碉楼、中山纪念堂、南越王博物院（王墓展区）、陈家祠。

（二）导游规范

主要考查考生在接待过程中向旅游者提供规范化、程序化服务的水平。如：考生在整个考试过程中规范化的表现（包括语言、举止、接待程序和标准）。考生须回答一个相关问题。

（三）应变能力

主要测试考生在接待过程中处理应急事件和机智回答旅游者提出的疑难问题的能力。如：旅游安全事故、旅游者突发疾病以及不当言行等事件的处理。考生须回答一个相关问题。

（四）综合知识

主要考查考生对本省重要景点知识的掌握程度，以及对时政、经济、文化、入境便利化等方面的综合知识是否全面了解。考生须回答一个相关问题。

（五）口译（外语类考生）

主要考查考生在导游服务过程中的现场中外互译能力、口语水平。内容侧重于所考查的五个景点中的部分内容。每位考生"中译外"和"外译中"的试题各一题。

第二节　导游现场考试流程

一、考试科目及时间

1.考试科目：现场考试，分为"中文类"及"外语类"两类。

2.考试时间：以准考证上发布时间为准。

3.考试用时：

"中文类"每场考试总用时32分钟，包含2分钟景点讲解准备时间、15分钟答题时间、15分钟系统回放检查。

"外语类"每场考试总用时60分钟，包含2分钟景点讲解准备时间、29分钟答题时间、29分钟系统回放检查。

二、试题说明

1."中文类"考生考试试题包括"景点讲解""景点问答"和"知识问答"三部分，共7道题。

（1）第一部分"景点讲解"，共1题，总分值55。

"景点讲解"总用时14分钟，其中：

☆准备时间为2分钟。

☆系统自动抽取景点，考生进行讲解准备，考生答题时间为6分钟。

☆答题结束后，系统自动回放检查6分钟。

（2）第二部分"景点问答"，共3题，每题5分，总分值15。

"景点问答"总用时6分钟，其中：

☆第1题：考生答题时间为1分钟，答题结束后，系统自动回放检查1分钟。

☆第2题：考生答题时间为1分钟，答题结束后，系统自动回放检查1分钟。

☆第3题：考生答题时间为1分钟，答题结束后，系统自动回放检查1分钟。

（3）第三部分"知识问答"，共3题。导游规范问答、应变能力问答及综合知识问答各1题。每题10分，总分值30。

"知识问答"总用时12分钟，其中：

☆导游规范问答：答题时间为2分钟，答题结束后，系统自动回放检查2分钟。

☆应变能力问答：答题时间为2分钟，答题结束后，系统自动回放检查2分钟。

☆综合知识问答：答题时间为2分钟，答题结束后，系统自动回放检查2分钟。

2."外语类"考生考试试题包括"景点讲解""景点问答""口译"和"知识问答"四部分，共9道题。

（1）第一部分"景点讲解"，共1题，总分值41。

"景点讲解"总用时18分钟，其中：

☆准备时间为2分钟。

☆系统自动抽取景点，考生进行讲解准备，考生答题时间为8分钟。

☆答题结束后，系统自动回放检查8分钟。

（2）第二部分"景点问答"，共3题，每题3分，总分值9。

"景点问答"总用时12分钟，其中：

☆第1题：考生答题时间为2分钟，答题结束后，系统自动回放检查2分钟。

☆第2题：考生答题时间为2分钟，答题结束后，系统自动回放检查2分钟。

☆第3题：考生答题时间为2分钟，答题结束后，系统自动回放检查2分钟。

（3）第三部分"口译"，共2题。中译外和外译中各1题，每题10分，总分值20。

"口译"总用时12分钟，其中：

☆中译外：答题时间为3分钟，答题结束后，系统自动回放检查3分钟。

☆外译中：答题时间为3分钟，答题结束后，系统自动回放检查3分钟。

（4）第四部分"知识问答"，共3题。导游规范问答、应变能力问答及综合知识问答各1题，每题10分，总分值30。

"知识问答"总用时18分钟，其中：

☆导游规范问答：答题时间为3分钟，答题结束后，系统自动回放检查3分钟。

☆应变能力问答：答题时间为3分钟，答题结束后，系统自动回放检查3分钟。

☆综合知识问答：答题时间为3分钟，答题结束后，系统自动回放检查3分钟。

三、答题方式

闭卷，所有试题通过计算机完成答题，考生在计算机上录制视频作答。

四、答题注意事项

（一）设备调试

1.考试开始前，考生输入准考证号登录考试系统，进入设备调试界面。

2.在"听音测试"界面点击"开始试音"按钮，检查耳麦听音是否正常。

3.在完成试音后，点击"下一步"进入"录制测试"界面。

4.依次点击"开始录制""结束录制""回放视频"按钮调试摄像头位置和检查耳麦听录是否正常，如不能正常使用可举手示意。

5.调试结束后，点击"下一步"进入等待考试开始界面。

（二）答题

考生答题无需进行其他操作，均由系统自动切换。

注意：考生只能按试题顺序进行答题，不可选题，离开当前试题后将无法返回作答。考生答题时，需保证整个考试录像过程中，头部位于视频窗口正中央，不可将头部置于视频窗口一侧或角落。

请扫二维码阅读更详尽的
机考系统操作指南

第三节　导游现场考试注意事项

一、仪容仪表要求

（一）面容要求

面容的总体要求是端正庄重、整洁干净、简约朴实、得体自然。具体要求如下：

1.男性保持干净整洁，不蓄胡须，鼻毛不外现。

2.女性以裸妆为宜，整体妆容保持清新、自然、柔和、淡雅。

（二）发型要求

1.男性的发型发式，一般要求干净利落、整洁自然，不宜过长，但最好也不要剃光头。基本的要求是"前发不覆额，侧发不掩耳，后发不过领"。

2.女性发型的总体要求是清爽利落、美观大方，不要披头散发、发饰过多。

3.发色以自然为主，尽量不染发。

（三）服饰要求

总体要求是端庄得体、干练稳重、朴素大方、温文尔雅。建议避免穿高领、臃肿、颜色深沉的衣服。避免穿得过于随意或花哨。过于休闲、运动或带有大量图案、亮片的服装可能会给他人留下不专业的印象，因此应避免穿着此类服装参加考试。

（四）配饰要求

1.耳环、项链以精巧为宜，不佩戴超过2件。

2.避免眼镜镜片产生反光。

3.避免佩戴可能影响考试或被视为作弊的物品，如耳机、墨镜、帽子等等。

二、仪态要求

（一）坐姿

坐姿端正，保证自己的肩部及以上部位在屏幕中，符合"考生须知"要求。

（二）表情

1.眼神

"眼语"是表情语的一种，十分重要。俗话说"眼睛是心灵的窗户"，眼神传达的情意，我们称之为"眼语"。运用"眼语"传情达意的原则是：友善、谦逊、真诚、坦然、自信。主动与游客（即考官）交流。避免翻白眼、眼神游离、挠头搔耳、挤眉弄眼等小动作。机考会抓拍一张照片，考生要注意面部细节。

眼神运用的技巧有：

☆点视法。目光注视某一对象，与之进行视线交流。使游客在心理上增加对你所讲解内容的兴趣，并感到一种被尊重的满足。

☆环视法。用视线从左到右或从前到后慢慢移动，扫视游客。这样可以与多位游客的眼神进行广泛的接触和交流。

☆虚视法。把自己80%的注意力集中在讲解内容，而非游客上。视线散成一片，"视而不见"，不集中在某一点上。

2.微笑

微笑是体现亲和力的重要手段，是导游诚心诚意为游客服务的内心反应。微笑要和讲解的具体内容、感情色彩、分寸合拍，还应依据场合、语境、传播对象的不同，恰当把握笑容的"度"。

（1）微笑运用的技巧：

☆一度微笑。嘴角两端微微上提，笑肌微抬，无须露齿。在服务场合，这种微笑最温和。

导游人员在准备进行讲解服务工作的时候、聆听游客诉求的时候、待岗的时候，运用"一度微笑"就恰到好处。所以，"一度微笑"最适合导游人员在准备阶段和与游客无直接接触时运用。

☆二度微笑。嘴角肌肉紧张，嘴角两端一起向上提，给上嘴唇施加上拉的紧张感，嘴角上扬15°左右，露出6颗牙齿左右。这种微笑表示鼓励、友好、礼貌。

当导游人员面对游客进行交流或开场讲解的时候，微笑由"一度微笑"上升为"二度微笑"即可。所以，"二度微笑"适用于与游客交流，比如问候、指引等场合。进行具体的服务内容时，采用"二度微笑"能够创造出更有亲和力的服务瞬间，例如在致欢迎词时："亲爱的游客朋友们，欢迎大家来到×××参观游览。"

☆三度微笑。拉紧肌肉使嘴角肌肉紧张，嘴角两端尽量上提，嘴角上扬30°，露出8颗上牙齿。

这种微笑是比较热情的表情语，表达祝贺、祝福，与熟悉的游客沟通时都可以采用"三度微笑"，这也是最富有情感、最能够感染游客的表情，例如在表达祝愿时："在此新春佳节之际，我们衷心祝愿所有的游客朋友们在新的一年里身体健康、事业兴旺、家庭和睦，笑口常开。愿广州的山水风光和人文气息给您留下深刻的印象和美好的回忆！"

（4）微笑训练的方法：

☆对着镜子微笑。找出自己最满意的笑容并不断训练，从不习惯微笑到习惯。

☆情绪记忆法。将生活中自己最好的情绪储存在记忆中，当需要微笑时，立即调动起当时的情绪，这时脸上就会露出笑容。

☆借助一些字词进行口形训练。微笑的口形为闭唇或微启唇，嘴角微向上翘。可借助一些字词发音时的口形来进行训练。如普通话中的"茄子""切切""姐姐""钱"等，默念这些字词时所形成的口形正好是微笑的最佳口形。

☆微笑时，说"E"，让嘴角朝后缩，微张双唇，这时可感觉到面部肌肉被拉向斜后上方；轻轻浅笑时，减少说"E"时嘴巴张开的幅度。相同的动作重复几次，直到感觉自然为止☆。

☆微笑与眼神、语言相结合。在微笑的时候，眼睛也要"微笑"，否则，给人的感觉是"皮笑肉不笑"。微笑着说"早上好""您好""欢迎来到×××景区参观游览"，不要光笑不说，或光说不笑。

（三）手势

导游讲解中的手势语言包括多种丰富而富有表现力的元素，它们不仅能够辅助口头表达，还能增强讲解的吸引力和感染力。

手势运用的原则为：规范、适时、准确、干净、利落；眼到、口到、手到；忌来回摆动、翘兰花指、捋头发、抓痒、频繁扶眼镜等。

讲解手势分为以下几类：

☆情意手势。这类手势主要用于表达导游在讲解过程中的情感，使讲解内容更加形象化、具体化。通过手势的起落、力度和速度的变化，导游能够传达出对景点的热爱、对历史的敬畏或是对故事的感慨，从而与游客建立更深的情感连接。

☆指示手势。指示手势是导游在讲解中最为常用的手势之一。主要用于指向具体的对象或方向，帮助游客更清晰地定位导游所描述的场景或事物。在指示时，导游应确保手势准确到位，避免产生歧义或误导游客。

☆象形手势。象形手势是一种模拟物体或景物形状的手势，通过手势的形状、大小和运动轨迹来模拟讲解中的具体事物。这种手势能够生动地展现景物的特点，使游客在脑海中形成更加直观的画面，加深对景点的印象。

三、讲解要求

（一）自然口语化与情感投入

在讲解时，务必保持自然流畅，仿佛在和朋友分享一次难忘的旅行经历。适当加入"啊""呢""对吧"等语气词，可以提升讲解的亲切感和生动性。同时，根据讲解内容的不同，适时调整情绪，让听众感受到你的热情与投入。比如，在描述壮丽山川时，声音可以更加激昂；而在讲述历史故事时，则可以适当放缓语速，让情感更加深沉。

（二）声音与语言的魅力展现

☆声音饱满。确保发音清晰有力，声音富有感染力，让每一个字都充满生命力。通过调整呼吸来保持声音的稳定性，避免过于尖锐或低沉。

☆情绪饱满。在讲解过程中，根据内容的变化，灵活运用声音的高低、快慢、轻重，营造出不同的氛围。比如，在介绍风景名胜时，可以提高音量，加快语速，展现出兴奋与期待；在讲述感人故事时，则可以降低音量，放慢语速，让听众感受到深厚的情感。

☆充满朝气与激情。始终保持积极向上的态度，用你的热情和活力感染每一位听众。通过适当的肢体语言（虽然机考中无法直接展现，但可以通过声音传达出这种感觉）和生动的描述，让听众仿佛身临其境。

（三）应对机考挑战

☆时间管理。在准备阶段，对讲解内容进行合理规划，确保在规定时间内完成讲解。可以设定时间节点进行模拟练习，以提高时间掌控能力。

☆知识准备。充分准备相关知识，包括景点历史、文化背景、特色活动等。遇到不会的问题时，保持冷静，尝试从已知信息中寻找线索，或运用类比、推理等方法进行回答。

☆自信表达。即使遇到意外情况或出错，也要保持自信，不要慌张。深呼吸，调整心态，继续以最佳状态完成讲解。记住，考官更看重的是你的应变能力和专业素养。

（四）掌握节奏与专注力

☆节奏掌控。在讲解过程中，根据内容的重要性和听众的反应，灵活调整讲解节奏。重要信息可以稍作停顿，让听众有时间消化。次要信息则可以快速带过，保持整体流程的连贯性。

☆专注力集中。无论周围环境如何变化，都要保持高度的专注力。将注意力完全集中在讲解内容上，忽略外界干扰。即使出现小错误或遗漏，也不要过分纠结，迅速调整心态继续讲解。

（五）综合运用

通过自然口语化的表达、声音与语言的魅力展现、有效的机考应对策略以及良好的节奏掌控与专注力，你将能够在导游词讲解中脱颖而出，给考官留下深刻印象。

四、考场纪律

1.开考前30分钟，考生凭本人纸质准考证和有效期内的身份证件原件进入考场，有效期内的身份证件必须和报名时所提交的有效证件一致。经监考人员核对无误后，由考场考务管理人员对考生逐一进行现场拍照。完成身份校验并签到后，对号入座，将准考证和身份证放置在桌面上。有效身份证件包括：中华人民共和国居民身份证、香港居民身份证、中国澳门特别行政区居民身份证、中华人民共和国港澳居民居住证、港澳地区居民来往内地通行证、中华人民共和国台湾居民居住证、台湾居民来往大陆通行证（台胞证）。

2.考生进入考场时，应将除准考证、身份证件之外的其他物品存放在监考人员指定的物品存放处（手机应关机），违者按违纪处理。考生入场后，在登录界面输入准考证号进行考试登录，并核对考试机屏幕显示的照片、姓名、性别、准考证号和身份证。

3.仔细阅读《考生须知》和《操作说明》，完成设备调试之后，等待考试开始。考生如发现信息有误，应举手向监考人员示意，并听从监考人员的安排进行现场登记处理。

4.考生应自觉遵守考场秩序，尊重考试工作人员，自觉接受监考人员的监督和检查，保持考场安静，遇到问题应举手向监考人员示意，不得以任何理由妨碍工作人员履行职责，不得扰乱考场秩序，不准在考场内吸烟或吃东西。

5.考试过程中，考生若出现发热、咳嗽、咽痛、胸痛、腹痛、呼吸困难、腹泻、呕吐等异常状况，应立即向监考人员举手示意。如果因突发疾病不能继续考试的，应当停止考试，立即就医。

6.考试过程中，考试机或其他考试设备若出现运行故障等异常情况，考生应举手示意，请监考人员帮助解决，不得自行处置。在异常情况处置期间，考生应在座位上安静等待，听从监考人员和考试工作人员的安排与引导。不允许监考或技术人员帮助操作考试界面，或对题意作解释、提示。严禁故意关机、自行重新启动计算机以及其他恶意操作行为。

7.正式开考后未在考试机上登录的考生，视为缺考，考试系统将不再接受该考生登录。

五、违纪情况处理规定

考生在考试期间违纪、违规的，按照《全国导游人员资格考试管理办法（试行）》第二十一条、第二十二条进行处理。

第二十一条　参加考试人员有以下情形之一，经监考老师提醒后不改正的，该科考试成绩按零分处理，并在一年内不得报名参加资格考试：

（一）在考试期间旁窥、交头接耳或者互打手势的；

（二）在考场或者其他禁止的范围内，喧哗、吸烟或者实施其他影响考场秩序的行为的；

（三）未按规定携带手机、信号接听器等电子通讯、存储、摄录设备的；

（四）将草稿纸等考试用纸带离考场的；

（五）未经考场工作人员同意在考试中擅自离开考场的；

（六）帮助他人作答，纵容他人抄袭的；

（七）抄袭与考试内容相关材料的；

（八）其他一般违纪违规行为。

第二十二条　参加考试人员有以下情形之一的，该科考试成绩按零分处理，并在两年内不得报名参加资格考试，导游从业人员存在以下违纪违规行为的，文化和旅游部将相关信息记入导游从业人员信息管理系统，并可注销该从业人员的资格证书，三年内不受理其报名申请：

（一）教唆或组织团伙作弊的；

（二）由他人冒名代替参加考试或者冒名代替他人参加考试的；

（三）使用摄录设备获取考试内容的；

（四）使用手机、手表等电子通讯、储存设备接听、接收、查看考试信息的；

（五）使用或提供伪造、涂改身份证件的；

（六）蓄意报复考试工作人员的；

（七）恶意操作导致考试无法正常运行的；

（八）其他严重违纪违规行为。

七、其他

1.考生须妥善保管好纸质准考证及电子打印件，以备考试和领取资格证时使用。考试当天考生如未携带纸质准考证，将不能进入考场。

2.因考站管理要求，考站不提供停车位，请考生尽量乘坐公共交通工具前往。

第二章
广东省省情介绍

【概况】

广东简称"粤",位于中国大陆最南部,是中国的南大门。东起汕头南澳县,西至湛江雷州市,北至韶关乐昌市,南至湛江徐闻县角尾乡登楼角。陆地面积17.98万平方千米,海域面积41.93万平方千米。截至2023年年末,广东省常住人口1亿2706万人,人口数量全国排名第一。

【气候】

广东省大部分地区属于亚热带季风气候,雨热同期,降水充沛。春季,广东各地鲜花盛开,是赏花观景的好时节。夏季虽也炎热,但得益于地理位置,相较于中国许多有"火炉"之名的城市,气候湿润,降水更加丰沛。进入秋季后,广东天气宜人,是欣赏自然风光和感受历史文化的好时机。而冬季的广东,更是逃离严寒、享受温暖阳光的理想选择。

【经济】

广东是目前中国经济第一大省。据统计,2023年广东省地区生产总值达到13.57万亿元,同比增长4.8%,是全国首个突破13万亿元的省份,经济总量连续35年居全国首位。

广东是改革开放的排头兵、先行地、实验区。党的十八大以来,习近平总书记曾三次到广东考察调研、两次参加全国两会广东代表团审议,就推动新时代改革开放发表一系列重要讲话,作出一系列重要指示,强调广东"在中国式现代化建设的大局中地位重要、作用突出"。

2023年4月,习近平总书记先后来到广东湛江、茂名、广州等地,深入企业、港口、农村等进行调研。这是党的十八大以来,习近平总书记第四次赴广东考察。这充分体现了总书记对广东工作的高度重视,对广东人民的关心厚爱,对广东发展的殷切期望。

【历史】

广东之所以称"粤",是因为广东古时为百越之地,"越""粤"同音,后来便以"粤"相称。广东历史源远流长,13万年前就有"马坝人"在今天的广东省韶关市曲江区繁衍生息。秦始皇统一中国之后,南北文化交流与民族融合日益密切。公元前214年,南海郡设立,郡治所在地"蕃禺"便位于现在的广州。唐代在广东、广西建置岭南道,北宋淳化四年(993年)更名为广南道,元代设广东道,明代设广东道宣慰使司,后改为广东布政使司,清代开设广东省,沿袭至今。

众多历史文化名人在广东留下了足迹。被毛主席誉为"南下干部第一人"的南越王赵佗,从担任秦朝的小县令到建立南越国,再到自去帝号归汉,促进汉越民族大融合,维护国家的统一,走完了他万古流芳的传奇一生。冼夫人一生为民族融合和国家统一的大业千里奔波,鞠躬尽瘁,不仅被尊称为"岭南圣母",还被周总理赞誉为"中国巾帼英雄第一人"。唐末著名诗人张九龄,在贬官返乡后倾力修建梅关古道,打通了中国南北交通命脉,使梅关成为"岭南第一关",被誉为"千古梅关第一人"。到了近现代,广东更是名人辈出,从领导农民起义的洪秀全,到布衣总统孙中山,再到文韬武略的叶剑英元帅……个个都如雷贯耳。

【方言】

广东省的语言复杂多样，方言数量众多，主要分布着粤、客、闽三大汉语方言。

粤方言又称粤语、白话等，是汉藏语系汉语族的一种声调语言，以广州话为标准音，拥有丰富的词汇和独特的语音特点，是广府文化的重要载体。粤方言广泛通行于中国广东中部、西南部及港澳地区，并影响东南亚及海外华人社区。粤方言保留了较多的古汉语成分，尤其是较为完整地保留了入声，被誉为语言史上的"活化石"。

客家方言简称客语，是汉藏语系汉语族的一种声调语言，也是汉语主要方言之一。它主要分布于广东的梅州、惠州、河源等地，以及江西、福建、台湾等省份的部分地区，甚至远播至海外多个国家和地区。客家话以其独特的语音、词汇和语法结构，成为客家民系的重要身份标识和文化传承的载体。

广东省闽方言包括潮汕话、雷州话以及闽南方言岛，又以粤东的潮汕话片区和粤西的雷州话片区为主。潮州话，又称潮汕话、潮语，属于闽南语系。它主要分布于广东的潮州、汕头、揭阳、汕尾等地区，并广泛流传于东南亚的潮人聚集区。潮州话保留了许多汉语的古音、古义，以其独特的语音系统和丰富的词汇成为潮汕地区文化的重要组成部分，是研究古汉语和潮汕文化的重要工具，也是潮汕人的重要沟通纽带和文化传承载体。

【文旅资源】

岭南文化兼收并蓄，博采众长，融汇了南越文化、中原文化和海洋文化。因此，广东人给许多人留下了务实、求新、求变的印象，广受赞誉。神奇的岭南大地，有着广府、客家、潮汕三大民系，有着古老独特的民俗民风。岭南四大名园、南越古驿道、广东省粤港澳大湾区文化遗产游径，以及西关骑楼、客家围屋、潮汕民居、开平碉楼等，都能让人清晰地感受到薪火相传的岭南文脉。

广东北枕五岭，南濒南海。这里的人们，世世代代在山海间繁衍生息，传承并发扬多姿多彩的非物质文化遗产。截至2024年8月，广东全省共有联合国教科文组织人类非遗代表作名录项目5项、国家级非遗代表性项目165项、省级非遗代表性项目816项。在广东，游客可以欣赏韵味十足的粤剧、潮剧、广东汉剧、雷剧，可以观看充满活力和英雄气概的舞狮、龙舟竞渡、英歌舞和武术表演，可以在旅途中，通过品尝、制作、聆听、观看、感触等多种方式，与经典非遗项目进行零距离接触，沉浸式感受非遗魅力。

说到中国最值得去的旅游胜地，广东肯定榜上有名。截至2024年8月，广东已经拥有15家国家5A级旅游景区、200多家4A级旅游景区。在这里，可以攀登丹霞山、罗浮山、西樵山、鼎湖山，游览肇庆星湖、惠州西湖和河源万绿湖等著名自然景观；可以漫步广州、潮州、佛山、惠州、肇庆等一众历史文化名城，感受那厚重的历史记忆与独特的文化韵味；可以在巽寮湾、海陵岛、南澳岛、放鸡岛，体验海洋的乐趣；可以畅玩长隆海洋王国、长隆欢乐世界、欢乐谷和融创乐园等大型主题公园。更令人瞩目的是，广东还拥有两大连接粤港澳三地的"超级工程"，一是世界最长的跨海大桥——港珠澳大桥，二是2024年正式通车试运营的深中通道。这两大工程不仅展现了中的科技实力，也成为广东旅游的新亮点。

广东是一片有着光荣革命历史传统的红色热土，是革命文物延续年代最长、序列最完整、种类最齐全的省份之一。这里有毛泽东同志主办农民运动讲习所旧址、广州起义烈士陵园、中共三大会址旧址、黄埔军校旧址纪念馆等革命遗址，让人仿佛穿越时空，亲身感受那段波澜壮阔的革命历史，深刻领悟革命先烈的崇高精神与伟大情怀。

广东是著名的华侨之乡。东莞、江门、潮汕一带都是远近闻名的华侨祖籍地。目前，祖籍广东的华侨华人3000多万，足迹遍及世界160多个国家和地区，对广东乃至全国的经济和社会发展作出了重大贡献。孙中山曾赞誉"华侨乃革命之母"，如今，广东还有许多名称含有"华侨"二字的学校、农场、宾馆、公司等。华侨文化作为岭南文化的特色和亮点，已成为推动广东旅游及经济发展的巨大力量。此外，广东华侨文化遗产丰富，中山的孙中山故居和孙文西街步行街、广州的上下九步行街、江门的开平碉楼、珠海的陈芳故居、汕头的陈慈黉故居、韶关的珠玑巷等，都成了当地的文化名片。

广东省内丘陵遍布，既可观赏奇险秀美的喀斯特地貌，又能领略极具岭南田园特色的水乡风情。顺德有逢简水乡，肇庆有金林水乡，江门有古劳水乡，中山有岭南水乡，每一处都展现了岭南人依水而居，与自然和谐共生的生活方式。漫步其间，仿佛回到那个宁静淳朴、诗意盎然的岭南水乡时代。

岭南园林是岭南建筑艺术的重要组成部分，也是中国园林三大流派之一。岭南园林代表作有广东四大古典名园——清晖园、余荫山房、可园、梁园，都是清代私家园林。岭南园林既继承了中国古典园林的传统，又受乡土文化和西方园艺的影响，其独特的风格对当代广州许多建筑的园林造景、绿化等方面有较大的影响，如白天鹅宾馆、花园酒店、中国大酒店、东方宾馆、矿泉别墅、白云山双溪别墅等。

建筑被称为凝固的史诗，最能代表一个城市的内涵。广东名胜古迹众多，岭南建筑往往与岭南园林有机结合，富有岭南传统文化的韵味，是非常有特色的一个建筑流派。以广州为代表的岭南建筑经历了四个发展阶段：第一阶段是明清时期的书院、祠堂建筑，如陈家祠和沙湾何氏宗祠等；第二阶段是清末民初的西关大屋、竹筒屋和商业骑楼建筑，如小画舫斋和广州城西骑楼街等；第三阶段是西洋建筑传入后，建筑师将中西建筑元素融合起来，如石室圣心大教堂和马丁堂等；第四阶段是中华人民共和国成立后，中西建筑艺术进一步融合，古为今用，洋为中用，岭南建筑逐渐进入现代化的发展阶段，形成具有鲜明地方特色的岭南派建筑新风格，如广州艺术博物院等。

【饮食文化】

俗话说"吃在广东"，粤菜是我国著名菜系之一，主要由广府菜、潮州菜、东江菜三种风味组成。

广府菜的著名菜肴有姜葱白切鸡、麻皮乳猪、脆皮烧鹅、红烧乳鸽、清汤鱼肚、八宝冬瓜盅、醋咕噜肉、麒麟生鱼、白云猪手等；小食大体可分为油器、粥品、粉面、糕品、甜品、粽子和什食七大类，价廉物美，遍布大街小巷。潮州菜简称潮菜，发源于潮汕平原，特点是普遍喜欢摆12款，上菜次序通常为头、尾甜菜，下半席上咸点心。客家菜偏重

"肥、咸、熟"，其中东江客家菜较为出名，主要代表菜式有东江盐焗鸡、东江酿豆腐、梅菜扣肉、八宝窝全鸭等。

2022年5月，"广府饮茶习俗"入选广东省人民政府第八批省级非物质文化遗产代表性项目名录。"得闲饮茶"是"老广"（即广东人）常说的一句话。广东人常说的"一盅两件"中，"一盅"通常指的是一壶热腾腾的铁观音或香浓的普洱，而"两件"则是指搭配茶水享用的点心，如虾饺、烧卖、肠粉等。在广东，饮食不仅仅是为了满足口腹之欲，更是一种社交方式，一种生活情趣的体现。人们围坐在一起，品茶尝点，谈笑风生，享受着一份独有的悠闲与惬意。

除此之外，广东人还很爱喝"凉茶"。由于岭南地区气温高、湿度大，从晋代葛洪编撰最早的"凉茶方子"开始，广东人充分发挥生活智慧，博取各家之长，推陈出新，逐渐形成了凉茶文化。"因时而食、四季皆宜"的凉茶成为广东人抵抗"春温，夏热，秋燥，冬寒"的"帮手"。2006年5月，凉茶还被国务院正式批准为首批国家级非物质文化遗产。

"宁可食无菜，不可食无汤。"汤文化早已融入广东人的血液，成为其生活不可或缺的一部分。广东的汤文化渗透了中华民族"食医合一"的饮食理念。汤源自中医药理的食疗良方"药汤"，不过真正的药汤实在太苦，于是酷爱美食的广东人在中药的煎熬中改良出了"老火汤"，使汤在保留原有功效的同时更加美味，逐渐演变为现在广为流传的日常汤食。

（数据来源：广东省人民政府网）

第三章
景点导游词精讲

第一节　广州市长隆旅游度假区

一、讲解要点

（一）概述

1.长隆旅游度假区的地位、美誉。

2.长隆旅游度假区的规模、主要景区。

（二）长隆野生动物世界

1.长隆野生动物世界的特色、珍稀动物、游览方式。

2.着重介绍某一园区及其动物。

3.长隆野生动物世界的其他特色设施。

二、中文讲解词示例

【欢迎词】

大家好！欢迎大家来到长隆旅游度假区！

【概述】

这里是中国拥有主题公园数量最多、规格最高的综合性主题旅游度假区，同时也是中国首批5A级旅游景区，国家文化产业示范基地、全国科普教育基地、国家旅游科技示范园区、国家级夜间文化和旅游消费集聚区。广州长隆旅游度假区被誉为"中国最受欢迎的一站式旅游度假胜地"和"广州城市名片"，曾作为亚洲唯一代表，夺得全球主题娱乐协会的"全球最佳主题乐园"前三名，实现了中国内地主题乐园在这一业内顶级大奖零的突破。2024年3月，长隆集团再获被誉为"全球主题乐园行业奥斯卡奖"的西娅奖的"杰出成就奖"。

整个度假区占地面积4平方千米，包括长隆野生动物世界、长隆欢乐世界、长隆酒店、长隆国际大马戏、长隆水上乐园、广州鳄鱼公园、香江大酒店、香江酒家等子公司。是能满足您吃、住、行、游、购、娱全方位体验的大型旅游度假区。

【长隆野生动物世界】

也许您去过很多动物园游玩，长隆野生动物世界和它们相比有什么不同呢？长隆野生动物世界园区占地面积达1.3平方千米，拥有大面积亚热带雨林原始生态，以大规模野生动物种群放养和自驾车、小火车、缆车观赏为特色，集动植物保护、科学研究、科普教育、文化旅游为一体，园内设有集讲解与动物于一身的动物科普驿站、内容丰富的科普长廊、生动有趣的动物学堂、充满温情的动物幼儿园。目前这里生活着15只国宝大熊猫，其中包括全球唯一存活的大熊猫三胞胎"萌萌""帅帅""酷酷"，还有八代同堂的68只澳洲考拉，是澳洲以外最大的考拉种群。长隆野生动物世界有150多只白老虎，还有马来西亚国宝黄猩猩、泰国国宝亚洲象、洪都拉斯国宝食蚁兽等500多种2万多只珍奇动物。长隆野生动物世界被世界动物园组织誉为"世界一流的野生动物园"。2023年5月，长隆野生动物世界入选国家林业和草原局、科学技术部公布的首批国家林草科普基地，为世界生物多样性提升和保护作出积极贡献。*技巧 讲解时可以和游客互动交流，和游客家乡的动物园进行对比。

　　动物世界分步行游览区和乘车游览区两个部分。步行游览区由青龙山、百虎山、猿猴王国、考拉园、大中华区、非洲部落、非洲森林、丛林发现等八大区域组成，以天鹅湖为中心，呈"左青龙右白虎"的布局，形成"风水宝地"。来自世界各地的珍稀动物和可爱的动物宝宝种类数量繁多，珍禽异兽在这里快乐生活。

【考拉园】

　　我们现在看到倚靠在树上睡得正香的小动物是考拉，考拉是澳洲国宝，又叫"树袋熊"，它有着圆滚滚的身体、一双竖着的带丛毛的耳朵、琥珀球似的小眼睛以及一个如黑橡胶做成的大鼻子。它们呆头笨脑、憨态十足的模样，获得了游客们的喜爱。

　　考拉最爱吃的食物是桉树叶，它有一个特别的消化器官——长达2米的盲肠，肠道内有着数以百万计的微生物，可以对桉树叶中的有毒物质进行消化分解，以此达到"解毒"的效果。然而，小考拉刚出生时肠道内并没有可以消化或吸收桉树叶的微生物，而需从母亲排泄的黏性流质粪便中获取。所以，考拉宝宝要食用这种特殊的"便便"来得到"解毒能力"。*技巧 在描述动物时，可通过生动的描述，融入对动物的尊重和喜爱之情，增加讲解的现场感和代入感。

【四大剧场】

　　在步行游览区还建有河马、花果山、白虎、大象四大剧场。每天的不同时段剧场都有精彩的表演，建议大家关注公众号及园区内的电子显示屏，以便及时了解演出时间安排。

【观光小火车】

　　乘车游览区有全国首创的"与兽同行"自驾车观赏野生动物模式，也可以乘坐小火车游览，现在让我们一起登上小火车，体验与动物近距离接触之旅。旅程中请大家注意自身以及动物安全，不要将头和手伸出车厢外，请勿擅自投喂。我们将看到袋鼠奔跑、驼羊漫步，感受成群的剑羚狂奔，仰望威武的狮群镇山而坐，遥看成群的斑马、角马在开阔的草原上穿行，还有"草原模特"长颈鹿在优雅地漫步。*技巧 在乘车游览区部分，应强调游客在观赏动物时需要注意的安全事项。

【结束语】

　　除了步行和乘坐小火车游览，我们还可以乘坐缆车从空中俯瞰园区。缆车分为非洲草原线路和天鹅湖线路，大家可以根据自己的需要选择游览方式。我的讲解到此结束，祝大家游玩愉快！谢谢！

三、英文讲解词示例

Guangzhou Chimelong Tourist Resort

Hello everyone, I am your guide for today's tour. First of all, welcome you all to Guangzhou Chimelong Tourist Resort!

It is the highest-scale theme resort with the largest number of theme parks in China. When it was completed and opened to the public, it became the first batch of National 5A Scenic Area, one of the Cultural Industry Demonstration Bases at the National Level, a National Science Popularization Education Base, one of the National Tourism and Technology Demonstration Zones, and the National Night Culture and Tourism Consumption Gathering Area. The resort was once known as one of the most popular one-stop tourist resorts in China and a name card of Guangzhou. Also, it was the only representative in Asia, ranking top 3 in The Best Theme Park in the World by Themed Entertainment Association. This was a great breakthrough in the whole industry for the domestic market. In March 2024, Chimelong Group was honored with the "Outstanding Achievement Award" at the THEA Award for the global theme park industry by the Themed Entertainment Association.

The whole resort covers an area of 4 square kilometers, including Chimelong Safari Park, Chimelong Paradise, Chimelong Hotel, Chimelong International Circus, Chimelong Water Park, Crocopark Guangzhou, Xiangjiang Hotel, Xiangjiang Restaurant and other subsidiary corporations. It is a large-scale tourist resort that can satisfy your needs of dinning out, staying at a hotel, traveling, shopping and entertaining in an all-round way.

I believe that the zoo is a quite common place for families or friends to go to. Then what are the differences about the Chimelong Safari Park?

The Chimelong Safari Park covers an area of 1.3 square kilometers, with a large area of subtropical rainforest primitive ecology. Animals are free to go wherever they like in the park and visitors can enter the park by driving private cars, taking tour trains or cable cars. It integrates animal and plant conservation, scientific research, science education, and cultural tourism into the visiting. Also, there are science stations explaining knowledge of animals, a science corridor with rich content, a lively and interesting animal school, and an animal kindergarten. Currently, there are 15 pandas living in the park, including the world's only surviving triplets panda Mengmeng, Shuaishuai, and Kuku. 68 Australian koalas live here and they are a big family tree which stretches for eight generations. They are the largest koala population outside Australia. Besides, more than 150 white tigers stay in the park. In total, there are more than 20,000 rare animals of 500 species living here, including the Orangutan of Malaysia, the Elephas maximus of Thailand, and the Anteater of Honduras. With such diverse resources and good care of animals, the park is listed as "The World-Class Safari Park" by the World Association of Zoos and Aquariums. In May 2023, it was selected into the first batch of the National Forest and Science Popularization Base announced by the National Forestry and Grassland Administration and the Ministry of Science and Technology, exerting positive influences to the improvement and conservation of global biodiversity.

The Safari Park is divided into a walking tour route and a car tour route. The former consists of 8 parts: Green Dragon Hill, Tiger Hill, Monkey Kingdom, Koala Zone, Greater China Area, African Tribe, African Forest, and Jungle. With the Swan Lake as the center, the layout of the green dragon hill on the left and the white tiger hill on the right forms a wonderful "Feng Shui" pattern.

The cute little animal here is koala, the national treasure of Australia. They are always in slow motion. It is a very charming point to all the tourists.

The koalas' favorite food is eucalyptus leaves. The eucalyptus leaves are toxic. Then why do koalas still choose it as their food? This is because of their special digestive organ— up to 2 meters of cecum. Their cecum has millions of microorganisms, helping koalas to digest the toxic substances in the leaves. It can be called a detoxification process. However, the detoxification power isn't born with koalas. For baby koalas, they don't have this power as their cecum has not been fully developed. They need the microorganisms to digest the leaves. How can they do it? They can only gain microorganisms from mother koala. That is, eating their mom's "poop". No worries, it is a special poop that can help baby koalas to detoxify the toxic leaves.

Along the walking tour route, there are four theaters: Hippo Theater, Monkey Hill Theater, White Tiger Theater, and Elephant Theater. There are wonderful performances in theaters at different times every day. If you are interested, please check the schedule on the display screen in the park or the official account.

The park is the first zoo to adopt the self-driving car visiting mode at the national level. We can also take a scenic train ride through. Now we are taking the train for the visit. In this way, we can watch free wild animals closely. Please pay attention to your own safety. During the journey, it is expected to see kangaroos jumping, llamas wondering, lions roaring, zebras crowding, wildebeests passing through, and the giraffes roaming.

If you are thinking that there are more ways to visit the park, the answer is yes! We can also take a cable car to see the park from the air. The cable car is divided into two routes. You can choose the most suitable one after reading the detailed information. This is the end of my explanation for today's tour. Hope you enjoy the view! Thank you for your time!

四、综合知识

☆2007年，中国第一批5A级旅游景区名单出炉，全国有66家旅游景区上榜，广东仅有两家，长隆旅游度假区就是其中一家，是中国拥有主题公园数量最多，规格最高的综合性主题旅游度假区。

☆长隆野生动物世界1997年开业，是中国第一批开业的民营野生动物主题公园，也是目前全球动物种群最多、最大的野生动物主题公园之一，生活着500多种2万多只珍奇动物。

☆长隆旅游度假区是国家文化和旅游部的文化产业示范基地、广东省的科普教育基地、广州市第一批重点文化产业园。2023年5月，长隆野生动物世界入选国家林业和草原局、科学技术部公布的首批国家林草科普基地。

☆长隆野生动物世界生活着15只国宝大熊猫，其中包括全球唯一存活的大熊猫三胞胎"萌萌""帅帅""酷酷"。三胞胎于2014年7月29日诞生，并在2024年7月29日的十周岁庆生活动上被吉尼斯世界纪录大中华区代表现场授予"首例繁殖成功的大熊猫三胞胎""最长寿的大熊猫三胞胎"两项认证。

☆2024年6月18日，三胞胎中的大姐"萌萌"顺利产下一胎雌性幼仔，"萌萌"也是中国大熊猫保护研究中心2024年的第一个"熊妈"。"萌萌"的丈夫是来自四川的"家和"。这位"上门女婿"刚被安排到"萌萌"的隔壁房间，"萌萌"就率先产生恋爱反应，主动追随对方的脚步，发出"咩咩"的叫声。雌性首先发情，这是大熊猫的自然规律。不久后"家和"隔网对叫，相互追随，就是两熊互生爱意，两情相悦了。

☆2013年，长隆成功繁育的首只大熊猫，也是在华南地区诞生的首只大熊猫"隆隆"诞生。2018年，"隆隆"顺利产下雄性幼仔一只，意味着广州土生土长的大熊猫迎来了第二代成员。一般大熊猫产后两三天才开始进食，而"隆隆"在生完两小时后就开始吃竹笋，这都得益于一直以来在长隆受到很好的照顾，身体条件非常好。"坐月子"期间，"隆隆"主要进食云南甜竹竹笋，长隆多年来大面积栽种，保证一年四季都可以供应新鲜可口的竹子。

☆长隆野生动物世界里八代同堂的68只澳洲考拉，是澳洲以外最大的考拉种群。2006年，首批6只考拉住进考拉园，同年初代考拉"淘淘"便生下全球唯一的考拉双胞胎"欢欢"和"乐乐"。第八代考拉"小叶子"出生于2022年6月，2023年4月25日至6月15日，广州长隆野生动物世界还举行了"超级考拉节"，庆祝"小叶子"第一次与游客见面。

☆长隆野生动物世界的乘车游览区采用全国首创的"与兽同行"观赏模式，游客可通过驾车或乘坐园内的缆车、小火车观赏大规模放养的大象、长颈鹿、斑马等野生动物。

☆长隆野生动物世界步行游览区建有河马、花果山、白虎、大象四大剧场。以天鹅湖为中心，"左青龙右白虎"的布局，形成"风水宝地"。

☆白虎是长隆野生动物世界的"镇园之宝"，也是长隆集团的吉祥物。目前，长隆野生动物世界已经拥有150多只白虎。除了白虎，园内还有华南虎、金虎、银虎以及孟加拉虎和东北虎，六大虎种总计300多只。百虎山内的每个虎种有自己的单独生活区域，生活区模拟老虎的野外生活环境，老虎体型、生活环境、生活习性不同，场馆的设计建设也就不同，十分"虎"性化。

☆长隆欢乐世界采用欧陆风格设计，开创国内欧陆式游乐园模式的先河。园区内引进了荣获吉尼斯世界纪录，全球第二台、亚洲首台的十环过山车。还有东半球唯一的摩托过山车、亚洲独一无二的U型滑板、拥有"全球过山车之王"称号的垂直过山车、合家欢的飞马家庭过山车等世界先进的游乐设备。

☆2011年，长隆欢乐世界推出首届"长隆欢乐玩圣节"，创下单日接待游客量达到10万人次的中国主题公园单日入园新纪录。在每年持续20多天的"玩圣节"期间，有巨型花车巡游、街头表演、电音派对等一系列演出节目，集声光乐特效和高科技于一体。

☆长隆水上乐园引进的全球首台"摇滚巨轮"玩水设备，最高达26米，三条滑道自带动力系统，可自主旋转，为游客带来快速前进、回转、倒后等一系列前所未有的玩水体验。

☆长隆水上乐园最受欢迎项目是"超级大喇叭"，它荣获国际旅游行业2006年度"最佳新项目金票奖"。

☆长隆水上乐园创新性打造"长隆水上电音节"，邀请知名艺人登台演出。主舞台设置了立体音声场系统、喷气枪、气泡烟雾等设施，打造演唱会级别的声光电效果。

☆长隆飞鸟乐园推出乘船探秘等寓教于乐的观鸟方式，集鸟类观赏和科普教育于一体。游客可在游船上一边听科普导游讲解，一边近距离观赏来自世界五大洲30多种近千只珍稀鸟类。

☆长隆飞鸟乐园开放鸟类繁育中心，游客可观察不同日龄的鸟蛋内部发育情况，园区还根据动物的繁殖期展示不同的鸟宝宝育婴实况，开放了后场的鸟蛋孵化、人工育幼、动物饲养、食物配给、动物治疗等全生命历程的参观。

☆长隆飞鸟乐园荟萃世界各地三百多种、上万只珍稀鸟类，除了丹顶鹤、黑天鹅、红腹锦鸡等各类珍禽，还拥有中国最大的火烈鸟种群和华南最大的朱鹮种群。

☆长隆飞鸟乐园不断在世界珍稀鸟类繁育上实现零的突破，已经掌握国际先进的鸟类繁育技术。曾一度全球仅剩7只的国宝朱鹮也在长隆成功繁育，已形成150多只的华南最大种群。

☆长隆独创了"白天看动物，晚上看马戏，住宿在动物主题酒店"的文化旅游模式。长隆酒店是中国首家动物生态主题及会展酒店。酒店拥有放养白虎、鹤、鹦鹉等动物的动物岛，游客可在白虎、火烈鸟等动物的陪伴下享受美食。

广州市长隆旅游度假区

概况

- 地位: 中国主题公园数量最多、规格最高的主题旅游度假区
- 荣誉: 国家5A级旅游景区、国家文化产业示范基地、全国科普教育基地、国家旅游科技示范园区、国家级夜间文化和旅游消费集聚区
- 称号: "最受欢迎的一站式旅游度假胜地""广州城市名片"
- 成就: 全球最佳主题乐园前三名(亚洲唯一代表)、西娅奖的"杰出成就奖"
- 面积: 4平方千米
- 组成部分: 野生动物世界、欢乐世界、酒店、大马戏、水上乐园等

长隆野生动物世界

特色
- 面积: 1.3平方千米
- 生态: 亚热带雨林原始生态
- 观赏方式: 步行、自驾车、小火车、缆车
- 功能: 动植物保护、科研、科普教育、文化旅游
- 设施: 科普驿站、科普长廊、动物学堂、动物幼儿园

珍稀动物
- 大熊猫: 15只,含三胞胎"萌萌""帅帅""酷酷"
- 考拉: 68只,澳洲以外最大种群
- 白虎: 150多只
- 其他: 黄猩猩、亚洲象、食蚁兽等500多种2万多只

荣誉与贡献
- 世界一流的野生动物园
- 首批国家林草科普基地

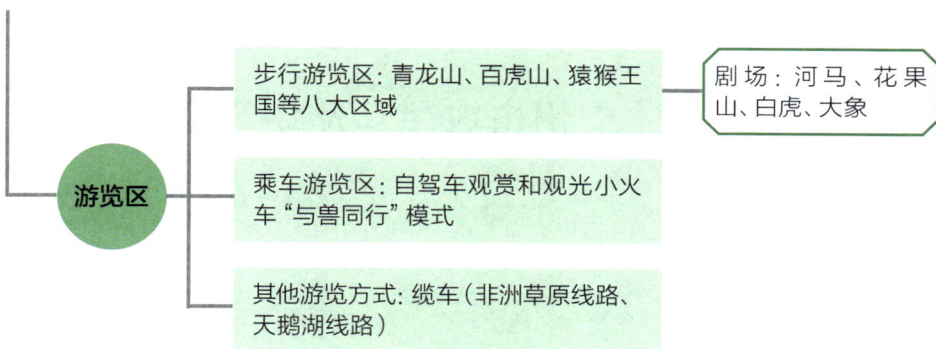

游览区
- 步行游览区：青龙山、百虎山、猿猴王国等八大区域 —— 剧场：河马、花果山、白虎、大象
- 乘车游览区：自驾车观赏和观光小火车"与兽同行"模式
- 其他游览方式：缆车（非洲草原线路、天鹅湖线路）

第二节　广州市农民运动讲习所旧址

一、讲解要点

（一）概述

1.广州农民运动讲习所的全称和地位。

2.农讲所的创办及影响。

3.第六届农讲所的三个"最"。

（二）"毛泽东主办第六届农讲所"陈列展

1.第六届农讲所的办学时间、学员人数及省区数。

2.国家一级文物：农讲所证章、周恩来题字、《中国农民问题丛刊》。

3.农讲所课程情况。

4.毛泽东、周恩来和萧楚女授课情况。

5.农讲所的两大教学特点。

二、中文讲解词示例

【欢迎词】

各位游客朋友们，大家好，欢迎参观广州农民运动讲习所旧址纪念馆。

【概述】

农讲所全称为"毛泽东同志主办农民运动讲习所旧址"，这十六个字是由周恩来亲笔题写的，如今就悬挂在农讲所的棂星门上。广州农讲所是全国重点文物保护单位、全国爱国主义教育示范基地、全国红色旅游经典景区，坐落在广州市越秀区中山四路。

在第一次国共合作时期，为唤起农民觉悟，在共产党人的倡议和主持下，从1924年7月至1926年9月连续举办了六届农民运动讲习所，一共培养了800多名学员。他们毕业后奔赴全国各地开展农民运动，将革命的火种散播开来，引燃革命燎原之火。*速记 办学时长和毕业人数：247；269；800。

第六届农讲所选址在占地宽广的番禺学宫，由毛泽东任所长，是历届办学规模最大，学习时间最长，影响最为深远的一届。*速记 三个最：最大，最长，最深远。

番禺学宫是古代的官办学府，始建于明洪武三年，即1370年，距今已有650多年历史。明清时期，这里是祭祀孔子的孔庙，也是生员求学的学宫。这座宏伟的古建筑，从南至北依次是棂星门、泮池拱桥、大成门、大成殿、崇圣殿。

【"毛泽东主办第六届农讲所"陈列展】

我们现在所处的大殿原是番禺学宫的崇圣殿，明清时期这里是供奉孔子先世五祖的地方，农讲所时期被设为膳堂，也就是饭堂。现在这里是农讲所的重要陈列："毛泽东主办第六届农讲所"展。

第六届的开办时间是1926年5月至9月，由毛泽东担任所长，他是中共党内较早认识到农民问题的重要性并付诸实践的领导人。

这里展示了第六届农讲所的学员籍贯表。第六届农讲所扩大招生范围至全国20个省区，一共招收了327名学生，是历届当中规模最大的。以外省籍学员为主，其中广西籍人数最多，有40名；广东籍学员仅有两名。

展柜内展示了两件国家一级文物，左边这件是第六届学员解学海的农讲所证章；右边这件则是周恩来在1953年亲自题写的馆名"毛泽东同志主办农民运动讲习所旧址"，这幅字也是农讲所的镇馆之宝。

【教员】

第六届农讲所共有21名教员，一共开设了25门理论课程，其中有关农民问题和农民运动的多达8门。接下来我为您介绍其中的几位教员。*速记 21位教员，25门课程，其中8门关于中国农民问题和农民运动。

毛泽东所长，除了负责所务外还亲自授课。他给学员讲授"中国农民问题""农村教育"和"地理"三门课程。其中"中国农民问题"是学生学习的中心内容，课时达23小时，是所有课程之最。*速记 农（中国农民问题）育（农村教育）地（地理）。

周恩来担任第六届农讲所军事训练部的军事教员。他给学员们讲授"军事运动与农民运动"。

萧楚女是第六届农讲所唯一的专职教员，讲授"帝国主义""社会问题与社会主义"等课程。他是一位非常让人敬重的老师，即使身患重病仍坚持讲课。他曾说："同学们，做人要像蜡烛一样，在有限的一生中，有一份热，发一份光，给人以光明，给人以温暖。"这是值得我们学习的"蜡烛人生观"。

展厅中央播放着影像，展示的是毛泽东在讲授《中国社会各阶级分析》时，形象地把阶级压迫比作多层宝塔的情景，他说："压迫、剥削阶级虽然很凶，但人数很少。只要大家齐心，团结紧，劳苦大众起来斗争，压在工农身上的几重大山就可推翻。"这篇文章后来作为开卷篇被收入《毛泽东选集》。

下方展柜展出的，是毛泽东担任所长期间主编的《农民问题丛刊》，现为国家一级文物。他在序言中明确指出："农民问题乃国民革命的中心问题，农民不起来参加并拥护国民革命，国民革命不会成功。"

【教学特点】

农讲所有两大教学特点：第一是坚持政治教育与军事训练并重的教学方针，军事训练内容占了课程的三分之一；第二是重视理论联系实际，将课堂教学与社会实践紧密结合，如带领学员到海丰农村实习。

【油画《送学员》】

1926年9月11日，第六届农讲所学员经过考试，有318人获准毕业，油画《送学员》描绘的是学员毕业时送学员的场景。中间穿长衫这位是所长毛泽东，旁边这位身穿军装的是军事教员周恩来，右边的三位分别是"农民运动大王"彭湃、第三届农讲所主任阮啸仙以及专职教员萧楚女。

【结束语】

学员们毕业了，我的讲解到这里也结束了，感谢大家的聆听！接下来的时间留给大家自由参观学习。谢谢大家！

三、英文讲解词示例

The Former Site of Guangzhou Peasant Movement Institute

Hi everyone! Welcome to the former site of Guangzhou Peasant Movement Institute.

The full name is "The Former Site of Peasant Movement Institute Directed by Comrade Mao Zedong". The name comprised of 16 Chinese characters was written by Zhou Enlai. The plaque hangs on Lingxing Gate. Guangzhou Peasant Movement Institute is selected as the Major Historical and Cultural Sites Protected at the National Level, National Demonstration Bases for Patriotism Education and National Red Tourism Scenic Area. It is located in No.4 Zhongshan Road, Yuexiu District, Guangzhou.

During the first cooperation between the Chinese Kuomintang Party and the Communist Party of China, or CPC, in the early-mid-1920s, CPC members suggested to raise farmers' awareness. Under the leadership of the CPC, from July 1924 to September 1926, there were a total of 6 classes or terms held in the Peasant Movement Institute, with over 800 young idealists being trained. After graduation, they went to all parts of China to carry out peasant movement, bringing the dream and passion for revolution to the whole nation. All these have contributed to revolution in China.

The 6th term of training was located in spacious Panyu Academic Palace, with Mao Zedong as the head. It was the largest class with the longest duration and greatest influence among all classes.

Panyu Academic Palace was an ancient government-funded school. Built in 1370, now it has a history of over 650 years. In the Ming Dynasty and Qing Dynasty, it was a Confucian temple to worship Confucius and a school for Xiucai. Xiucai means a scholar who has passed the entry-level examination to study at a college. In this magnificent ancient building, one can see Lingxing Gate, a semicircle pool and an arch bridge over it, Dacheng Gate, Dacheng Hall and Chongsheng Hall lying from south to north.

Now we are standing in front of the main hall, the previous Chongsheng Hall in Panyu Academic Palace. In the Ming and Qing Dynasty, it was used to worship the ancestors of Confucius. From 1924 to 1926, it was the canteen for trainers and students. Now there is an important exhibition here: *Mao Zedong Organized the 6th Term of Peasant Movement Training.*

The 6th term started from May to September in 1926, with Mao Zedong as the director. He was the CPC leader who recognized the importance of peasant issues and took concrete action to solve them at an early time.

Here shows the list of birth place of students in the 6th term. In total, there were 327 students who were from 20 provinces in China. It was the largest size among all terms. Most of them were non-Cantonese students. There were over 40 students from Guangxi Province, accounting for the largest share. And only two students were from Guangdong.

There are two First Grade Cultural Relics in this showcase. The left one is Xie Xuehai's badge of Peasant Movement Institute. The right one is the calligraphy work "The Former Site of Peasant Movement Institute Directed by Comrade Mao Zedong" by Zhou Enlai in 1953. This calligraphy work is also the key highlight of the collections.

There were 21 lecturers in the 6th term with 25 theoretical courses. 8 of them were related to farmers' issues and peasant movement. Please allow me to introduce several lecturers:

Mao Zedong, the head of the institute. He was in charge of daily routine and training. He lectured on three courses: *Issues of Chinese Peasants, Education in Rural Areas* and *Geography. Issues of Chinese Peasants* were the core part of the whole term. It had 23 class hours in total, the longest one of all courses.

Zhou Enlai was the lecturer of military training department of the 6th term. He lectured on *Military Movement and Peasant Movement.*

Xiao Chunv was the only full-time lecturer in the 6th term of Peasant Movement Institute. He lectured on *Imperialism* and *Social Issues and Socialism*. He was a respectable teacher. Even with serious diseases, he still continued with his class. He once said: "In one's limited lifetime, a person should live like a candle giving light and warmth to other people." This is the spirit that deserves our admiration and learning.

In the video shown in the exhibition hall, we can see that Comrade Mao Zedong is lecturing on *Analysis of All Classes of Chinese Society*. He vividly compared class oppression to multi-storied pagoda. He said exploiting class were brutal and barbaric, but the number of them was very limited. As long as the poor peasants and workers united together and fought against them, they could overthrow several heavy burdens laid on most of the ordinary Chinese people. This article is included in *Selected Works of Mao Zedong* as the first passage.

The showcase below displays the book *Journal of Peasants Issues*. Mao Zedong was the editor-in-chief when he served as the head of the institute. Now the book is the First Grade Cultural Relic. In foreword, he pointed out that "The issue of peasants is the core of the National Revolution. Without peasants' participation and support, the National Revolution will never succeed."

There were two characteristics in teaching. First, the teaching guideline attaches equal importance to political education and military training. The later one accounted for one third of the curriculum. Second, applied theories to practice. Lecturers closely integrated classroom teaching with social practice. For instance, they brought students to have internship in rural areas of Haifeng.

On September 11, 1926, all students in the 6th term took part in the exam and 318 of them successfully graduated. The oil painting Farewell shows the occasion of students graduation. The man in long gown standing in the middle is Comrade Mao Zedong. Next to him, the one in military uniform is Zhou Enlai, the military lecturer. Those three men standing on their right are Peng Pai, pioneer of peasant movement, Ruan Xiaoxian, the head of the 3rd term and full-time lecturer Xiao Chunv.

That's the end of my commentary. Thank you for listening! Now it is time for you to visit freely!

四、综合知识

☆第一次国共合作形成后，国民革命运动迅猛发展。"农民运动大王"彭湃认识到人才缺乏带来的制约，倡议开办农民运动讲习所。1924年7月3日，第一届农讲所正式开办，所址设在惠州会馆（现越秀南路93号的中华全国总工会旧址纪念馆）。

☆从1924年7月至1926年9月，一共举办了六届农讲所，相继由彭湃（第一和第五届）、罗绮园、阮啸仙、谭植棠、毛泽东主持。

☆1926年5月至9月，举办了第六届农讲所，毛泽东任所长，周恩来、萧楚女、彭湃、恽代英等共产党员任教员，共招收了来自20个省区的327名学员。所址在广州番禺学宫。第六届广州农讲所是规模最大，学习时间最长，影响最为深远的一届。

☆从第五届农讲所开始，农讲所学员须经过严格考试，招生条件也相对严格。在纪念馆陈列室陈列的《1926年通告各省派人来第六届农讲所学习》文件中，可以看到要求有"需中学程度，文理通顺，年龄十八至二十八岁"等。

☆农讲所学员依据广州办学模式在湖南、江西、湖北、广西等地创办地方性农讲所，故广州农讲所被称为"中国农讲所的母校"。

☆1953年，毛泽东同志主办农民运动讲习所旧址纪念馆建立，周恩来亲笔手书纪念馆馆名。1961年，它被列为第一批全国重点文物保护单位。旧址目前已按当年原貌恢复了所长办公室、教务部、军事训练部、课堂、学员宿舍等设施。据学员回忆，毛泽东当年所用物品非常简单朴素,床上用竹竿挂上粗布蚊帐,床头放两个储藏书报的湖南旧竹箱,仅此而已。

☆毛泽东除担任所长,负责主持所务工作外,还亲自给学生讲授了"中国农民问题""农村教育""地理"三门课程以及中国社会各阶级的分析专题。其中"中国农民问题"是学生学习的中心内容,课时达23小时,是所有课程之最。

☆毛泽东主编的《农民问题丛刊》,一共出版了26种,为农讲所学员以及全国各地的农运干部提供了丰富而宝贵的学习材料。丛刊第一辑出版时,毛泽东亲自为该丛刊撰写了序言《国民革命与农民运动》,指出:"农民问题乃国民革命的中心问题,农民不起来参加并拥护国民革命,国民革命不会成功。"

☆第六届农讲所还设立了军事训练部,由赵自选担任军事训练部主任和总队长。周恩来担任农讲所军事教员,讲授"军事运动与农民运动"。农讲所坚持政治教育与军事训练并重的教学方针,对学员进行严格的军事训练。每天早上军号一响,学员们迅速起床,到附近的东较场、黄花岗、白云山进行演练,也会去石井兵工厂进行实弹射击。

☆萧楚女是第六届农讲所唯一一位专职教员,主要负责农讲所的教务工作,讲授"帝国主义""社会问题与社会主义"等课程。他有一句名言:"做人要像蜡烛一样,在有限的一生中,有一份热,发一份光,给人以光明,给人以温暖。"萧楚女的"蜡烛人生观"正是千千万万共产党人初心的体现。

☆农讲所内,有一棵挺立190多年、浓荫蔽日的古龙眼树。开办农讲所期间,龙眼结果的时候,毛泽东曾经和学员们吃着树上结出的龙眼,聚在树荫下谈心,了解他们的学习收获,了解各地农民运动情况,掌握第一手调查资料。

☆唐贞观四年,朝廷"诏州县学皆作孔子庙",从此各州县学宫旁修建孔子庙,"庙学合一",学宫既是祭祀孔子的地方,也是学子求学的场所。目前,中国有千百座孔庙,只有山东曲阜孔子故里的曲阜孔庙和浙江衢州的衢州孔庙是家庙规制,其余的孔庙都是"庙学合一"的规制。

☆番禺学宫从南至北由棂星门、泮池、拱桥、大成门、大成殿、崇圣殿和两侧的两廊、两庑、明伦堂等组成。沿着大成殿两侧的通道向前走去,即达崇圣殿。崇圣殿原是供奉孔子先世五代的地方。举办农讲所期间,崇圣殿被当作学员的饭堂使用。

☆旧址纪念馆复原了一整套开笔礼仪式,每年接纳各地少年儿童慕名而来参与开笔。开笔礼仪式俗称"破蒙",是学宫传统文化的重要组成部分,表示少儿开始识字习礼,人生由此起步,体现了中华民族重视教育、追求科学文化知识、勇于探索客观世界真理的优良传统。

广州市农民运动讲习所旧址

概况

- **位置** —— 广州市越秀区中山四路
- **全称** —— 毛泽东同志主办农民运动讲习所旧址
- **地位** —— 全国重点文物保护单位、全国爱国主义教育示范基地、全国红色旅游经典景区
- **办学缘由** —— 唤起农民觉悟
- **办学时间**
  - 1924年7月—1926年9月，一共举办六届
  - 第六届，1926年5月—9月
- **办学地点**
  - 第一、二届: 越秀南路惠州会馆
  - 第三、四、五届: 东皋大道1号
  - 第六届: 番禺学宫
    - 建立时间: 明洪武三年（1370年）
    - 作用: 明清祭祀孔子、培养儒家生员的地方
    - 主要建筑: 棂星门、泮池拱桥、大成门、大成殿、崇圣殿

```mermaid
graph LR
    A["『毛泽东主办第六届农讲所』展"] --> B((地点))
    A --> C((办学情况))
    A --> D((展柜文物))
    A --> E((授课影像))

    B --> B1[崇圣殿]
    B --> B2[明清时期: 供奉孔子先世五祖]
    B --> B3[农讲所时期: 膳堂（饭堂）]

    C --> C1[招生规模: 全国20个省区，327人，外省籍为主]
    C --> C2[招生条件: 有意愿，中学文化，年龄18—28岁]
    C --> C3[教学特点]
    C3 --> C3a[政治教育与军事训练并重]
    C3 --> C3b[课堂教学与社会实践结合]
    C --> C4[教员: 21人]
    C4 --> C4a[所长毛泽东: 讲授"中国农民问题""农村教育""地理"]
    C4 --> C4b[萧楚女: 唯一专职教员，讲授"帝国主义""社会问题与社会主义"，蜡烛人生观]
    C4 --> C4c[周恩来: 军事教员，讲授"军事运动与农民运动"]
    C --> C5[毕业]
    C5 --> C5a[油画《送学员》]

    D --> D1[农讲所证章: 第六届学员解学海]
    D --> D2[馆名: "毛泽东同志主办农民运动讲习所旧址"，镇馆之宝，周恩来1953年亲自题写]
    D --> D3[《农民问题丛刊》: 毛泽东担任所长期间主编]

    E --> E1[毛泽东讲授《中国社会各阶级分析》，把阶级压迫比作多层宝塔]
```

三件国家一级文物

第三节　深圳市华侨城旅游度假区

一、讲解要点

（一）概述

1.深圳华侨城的创立时间及地位。

2.深圳华侨城的主要景区。

3.深圳华侨城的便利游览设施。

（二）锦绣中华

1.锦绣中华的美誉。

2.锦绣中华占地面积及微缩景点数量。

3.重点介绍"世界八大奇迹"及"中国与世界之最"。

（三）中国民俗文化村

1.民俗村的占地面积及建村原则。

2.民俗村的建筑比例及种类。

3.选择介绍几个有代表性的民族建筑。

4.民俗村的节目表演。

二、中文讲解词示例

【欢迎词】

各位游客朋友们大家好！今天，我来带领大家游览深圳华侨城旅游度假区。古人说："有朋自远方来，不亦乐乎？"首先，欢迎大家的到来，希望在我的陪伴下，大家接下来的游览可以听得有趣，玩得愉快，游得尽兴。

【概述】

来到深圳，大家一定不能错过锦绣中华、中国民俗文化村这些国内著名的主题景区，接下来，就让我们一起前往"深圳八景"之一的"侨城锦绣"，去探寻这些景点的魅力吧！

华侨城创立于1985年，是一个以文化旅游景区为主体、配套完善的旅游度假区。经过近40年的开发建设，区域内包括艺术馆、保龄球馆、高尔夫球俱乐部、大型购物广场、食街及五星级酒店等20多个旅游项目。并且自东至西将锦绣中华、中国民俗文化村、世界之窗、欢乐谷等大型文化主题公园串联起来，成为中国首批5A级旅游景区。虽然景点众多，但是各景点之间交通非常便利。景区内各个旅游点之间设有名为"欢乐干线"的循环式高架单轨列车，大家可以乘坐列车在各景点之间穿梭，既方便游览，又可以从空中俯瞰华侨城的整体景色，可谓一举多得。

【锦绣中华】

我们现在来到的是锦绣中华微缩景区，也叫"深圳小人国"。这是中国第一个微缩景区和主题公园，也是当时世界最大、最真实的微缩景区。锦绣中华景区于1987年破土动工，占地30万平方米，区内的80多个景观按中国版图位置分布，并以1：15比例复制，1989年正式对外开放。虽然景区开放距今已经35年，但时至今日，锦绣中华仍是非常值得参观的主题景区。"一步迈进历史，一日畅游中国"是锦绣中华微缩景区的生动写照，它集中反映了中国这个多民族国家风格迥异的建筑、生活习俗和风土人情。

【人文建筑和自然景观】

在这里您可以看到被称为"世界八大奇迹"的万里长城、秦陵兵马俑，还可以了解众多"中国与世界之最"：世界现存最古老的石拱桥——赵州桥，我国现存最古老的天文台——登封观星台，世界现存最高、最古老的木塔——应县木塔，世界上最大的宫殿建筑群——故宫。可以欣赏雄伟壮观的泰山、险峻挺拔的长江三峡、如诗如画的漓江山水，还可以看到肃穆庄严的黄帝陵、成吉思汗陵、明十三陵、中山陵，以及金碧辉煌的孔庙、天坛等祭祀建筑。总之，锦绣中华微缩景区可以让您在一天之内领略中华五千年历史风云、畅游大江南北、锦绣山河。

【中国民俗文化村】

参观完微缩景区里的著名景观，接下来，我将带领大家走进锦绣中华景区的另一片区域——中国民俗文化村，这里占地18万平方米，以"源于生活、高于生活、荟集精华、有所取舍"为建村的指导原则，和微缩景观不同的是，为了从不同角度反映我国多民族的民俗文化，景区按原景观的1：1比例，建有各具特色的村寨、庭院和街市，展示28个民族、56种风情。其中有个亮点就是，很多村寨中有本民族的村民进驻，真实地向各位游客展示他们民族的民俗文化。

【民族民居】

在这里，黎族的船形屋和佤族的杆栏式草楼相映成趣，再现了人类古老的建筑文化；白族雕刻精美的"三坊一照壁"和汉族的四合院，则表现了高水准的中国传统民居建筑设计工艺。布依族的石头寨、摩梭人的木楞房、哈尼族的蘑菇房、哈萨克族的毡房、蒙古族的蒙古包等无不吸引着大家走入建筑内仔细参观。而围绕在这些民居周围的则是成片的海南椰林、参天的西双版纳古榕、开屏的孔雀和漫步的大象。*技巧 可选择几个有代表性的民族建筑进行介绍。

【节目表演】

除了各具特色的村寨建筑，民俗村中还有80多个精彩节目，全部由当地民族演员表演。彝族的火把节、傣族的泼水节、回族的花儿会、傈僳族的刀杆节这些别具特色的大型民间节庆活动，也会在不同月份举行。在这里您还可以欣赏并参与各民族的歌舞表演，品尝民族风味食品，参观民俗陈列馆，体验特色民族工艺品制作等，总之，56个民族多姿多彩的文化艺术，您在这里都可以身临其境地参与到、体验到、了解到。

【结束语】

今天的锦绣中华和中国民俗文化村景区就为大家介绍到这里，祝大家游览愉快！

三、英文讲解词示例

Shenzhen Overseas Chinese Town Tourist Resort

Hello everyone, I am your guide for today's tour. First of all, welcome to Tourist Resort— Shenzhen Overseas Chinese Town, we can call it OCT for short. As an old saying goes in China, "How happy we are, to meet friends from afar!" Hope we will have a joyful, interesting and great journey together.

As we have arrived here, we can't miss the Splendid China, China Folk Culture Village and more wonderful themed parks of China. So now, we are heading towards to Splendid City in the Overseas Chinese Town, one of the Eight Scenic Spots in Shenzhen.

OCT Tourist Resort, founded in 1985, is a resort with cultural tourist attractions as its main part and complete supporting facilities. 40 years of planning and development have made the whole area cover more than 20 tourist spots, including art museums, a bowling alley, a golf club, a shopping mall, a food court, and a five-star hotel. From east to west, Splendid China, Chinese Folk Culture Village, Window of the World, Happy Valley and other large-scale cultural theme parks are connected, making it the first National 5A Scenic Area in China. With so many attractions, convenient transportation is what tourists need the most. Therefore, a circulating elevated monorail shuttle train named Happy Lines can take us to wherever spots we want. Moreover, it is a good opportunity to view the overall scenery of OCT from the air on the train.

Now we are at the Splendid China Miniature Park, also known as "Shenzhen Lilliput". It is China's first miniature scenic spot and theme park, also the world's largest and most realistic one at that time. With 300,000 square meters coverage, the park has over 80 scenic spots which were replicated according to the ratio 1:15. The replicated spots which were distributed in the park according to their geographical locations. The park was officially opened to the public in 1989. 35 years have passed, and Splendid China is still a good choice for tourists. "One step into the era, one day tour of China." is a vivid portrayal of the miniature park, which reflects the differences in architecture, customs, and lifestyles of various ethnic groups in China.

In the miniature world, we can see the Great Wall, Terracotta Warriors, two of the world's eight wonders; the arch bridge with the oldest stone—Zhaozhou Bridge, the oldest surviving astronomical observatory in China—Dengfeng Observatory, the highest, and the oldest wooden tower—Yingxian Wooden Tower, the largest palace complex—the Forbidden City, and other

China and the world's greatest scenic spots. What's more, we have the Mount Tai, Lijiang River, Huangdi Mausoleum, Mausoleum of Genghis Khan, Ming Tombs, Sun Yat-sen Mausoleum, Confucian Temple, Temple of Heaven, and more spectacular buildings. Just one day tour, 5,000 years of history, and a land of splendors are all grasped from here.

Now, we are heading to the Chinese Folk Culture Village, the other part consists of Splendid China. The whole area is 180,000 square meters. The guiding principle of the village is "Originating from life but beyond, Gathering the essence and discarding the gross." To reflect the folk culture, villages, courtyards, and streets with strong characteristics 28 nationalities were built according to the 1:1 ratio of the original landscape. This has greatly shown the profound and colorful life and features of China as a multinational country. Most importantly, people who are from these nationalities, display their authentic folk culture to our visitors.

As we can see here, these are the boat-shaped houses of the Li nationality and the Stilt house of the Wa nationality, showing the ancient architectural wisdom of mankind. Additionally, there are more wonders attracting visitors, including the exquisitely carved "three workshops a screen wall" of the Bai nationality and the Quadrangle courtyard of the Han nationality represent the high standard of Chinese traditional architectural designs. The stone village of Bouye nationality, the wooden house of Mosuo, the Hani mushroom house, the Mongolian yurt of the Mongol nationality and more characteristic houses are all attracting visitors to go inside the buildings.

Tourists not only can enjoy the distinctive views of village buildings, they can also immerse themselves in local culture by appreciating more than 80 wonderful shows in the village. All of the shows are performed by local actors and actresses. Large folk festivals with unique characteristics, such as the Torch Festival of the Yi people, the Water-Sprinkling Festival of the Dai people, the Flower Festival of the Hui people, and the Knifeladder-Climbing Festival of the Lisu people, are also held in different months. Also, you can enjoy and participate in the song and dance performances, taste authentic food, visit the folk museum, even make crafts with your own hands!

Hope you have a great journey for today and also take your time to experience here. Thank you for your time!

四、综合知识

☆华侨城旅游度假区创建于1985年，是一个以文化旅游景区为主体、配套完善的旅游度假区，区域内包括有艺术馆、保龄球馆、高尔夫球俱乐部、大型购物广场、食街及五星级酒店等20多个旅游项目。

☆2004年，华侨城旅游度假区被国家文化部授予首批全国文化产业示范基地；2006

年，被中央文明办、建设部、国家旅游局评为全国文明风景旅游区，这是中国旅游界的最高荣誉。2007年8月，又被文化部评为首批仅有的两家国家级文化产业示范园区之一。2007年，华侨城旅游度假区的世界之窗、锦绣中华民俗文化村、欢乐谷、阳光海岸景点被评为国家首批5A级旅游景区。

☆"深圳八景"分别为大鹏所城、莲山春早、侨城锦绣、深南溢彩、梧桐烟云、梅沙踏浪、一街两制、羊台叠翠，其中"侨城锦绣"指的就是华侨城旅游度假区。

☆深圳华侨城旅游度假区内设有名为"欢乐干线"的高架单轨列车，穿梭于各大旅游点和酒店之间，游人可从空中观赏华侨城的整体景色。

☆2024年5月，深圳华侨城旅游度假区举办"华侨城旅游狂欢节"，在度假区内各景区推出各类文化活动，包括古韵国风之约、非遗集市、民俗体验等，游客可参加木偶剧、儿童剧、音乐剧、艺术展览等文化艺术活动，在锦绣中华民俗村欣赏各朝代、各民族华服之美。此外，还有电音节、露营生活节、OCT凤凰花嘉年华，等等。

☆锦绣中华微缩景区也叫"深圳小人国"，是中国第一个微缩景区和主题公园，也是当时世界最大、最真实的微缩景区。大部分微缩景观按1：15比例复制。景区内80多个景点按中国版图位置分布，游客在游览时如同在巨大的中国地图上游走。"一步迈进历史，一日畅游中国"是锦绣中华微缩景区的生动写照。

☆锦绣中华微缩景区的景点可以分为三大类：古建筑类、山水名胜类、民居民俗类。古建筑类有入选"世界八大奇迹"、世界文化遗产的长城、秦陵兵马俑；有众多"中国与世界之最"：世界现存最古老的石拱桥——赵州桥，我国现存最古老的天文台——登封观星台，世界现存最高、最古老的木塔——应县木塔；世界上最大的宫殿建筑群——故宫。山水名胜类有世界文化与自然双重遗产、世界地质公园泰山，还有长江三峡、漓江、杭州西湖、苏州园林等。民居民俗类主要包括具有民族风情的地方民居，以及皇帝祭天、孔庙祭典的景观与民间的婚丧嫁娶风俗。

☆赵州桥位于河北省石家庄市赵县洨河之上，始建于隋代，距今已有1400多年历史，是世界现存最早、跨度最大的单孔圆弧敞肩石拱桥。全长64.4米，自建成之日起就作为交通要道使用，直到1984年营建赵州桥公园后才停用。赵州桥能屹立至今的主要原因是其出色的设计，主拱两端设有四个小拱，这些小拱不仅能够节约材料，减少桥梁自重，还可减少洪水对桥梁本体的冲击。

☆登封观星台位于登封城东南的告城镇周公庙内，始建于元至元十三年（1276年）。当时元世祖忽必烈为了恢复战后的农业生产，命令著名科学家郭守敬和王恂等进行历法改革，在全国二十七个地方建立了天文台和观测站，登封观星台就是当时的中心观测站。观星台由台身和石圭组成，石圭用来度量日影长短，所以又称"量天尺"。

☆应县木塔位于山西省朔州市应县，始建于辽清宁二年（1056年），全名"佛宫寺释迦塔"，是一座八角五层的楼阁式木塔。应县木塔是我国木建筑结构的集大成者，光是斗拱就有54种。20世纪30年代，我国著名建筑家梁思成先生和莫宗江先生，用了两个星期对应县木塔所有木构件进行测绘。古代工匠杰出的建筑技术，使应县木塔抵挡住了900多年的多次地震，唐山大地震时，这里的烈度也有4级。20世纪20年代军阀混战，应县木塔在战火中也坚持了下来，现在塔身上还有大量弹痕。如今应县木塔因为倾斜，2010年后已不准游客登塔。

☆中国民俗文化村内有28个民族的村寨，按1∶1比例建成，有"中国民俗博物馆"之称。景区以"源于生活，高于生活，荟萃精华，有所取舍"为建村原则，荟萃各民族民间艺术、民俗风情和民居建筑于一园，有布依族的石头寨、摩梭人的木楞房、哈尼族的蘑菇房、傣族的竹楼、土家族的水上街市、蒙古族的蒙古包、彝族的土掌房，等等。还有手工作坊以及民间手工艺和民间小吃的制作表演，如维吾尔族手绣、苗族蜡染、傣族竹筒饭等。

☆近年来，锦绣中华民俗村还打造了傣族泼水节、苗族芦笙节、华夏民族大庙会、新疆文化风情节、蒙古人草原文化风情节、中国功夫节、迷情聊斋夜等节庆活动，平均每年举办节庆活动2000多场次。

☆1992年，邓小平视察深圳时参观锦绣中华民俗村，在布达拉宫景点与家人留下珍贵的合影。布达拉宫是西藏现存最大的宫堡式建筑群，融合了藏、汉、满等民族的建筑工艺和审美风格，是世界文化遗产、国家5A级旅游景区。

☆深圳欢乐谷于1998年开业，以"体验即生活，生活就是体验"为设计理念，已成为国内投资规模最大、设施最先进的现代主题乐园。深圳欢乐谷共接待海内外游客超过6000万人次，曾连续8年位居国内第一，并连续四年荣膺亚太十大主题公园。

☆欢乐谷分为九大主题区，共有100多个游乐项目。有中国第一个高空摇摆项目"发现者"大摆锤、亚洲第一的家庭骑乘类项目"UFO"、世界最先进的高空直落项目"尖峰时刻"、亚洲首座集视觉、听觉、触觉于一体的四维影院，等等。

☆深圳世界之窗于1994年建成，由世界广场、亚洲区、大洋洲区、欧洲区、非洲区、美洲区、世界雕塑园、国际街八大区域构成，有以缩小比例仿建的世界景点130多个，其中包括世界著名景观埃及金字塔、阿蒙神庙、柬埔寨吴哥窟、美国大峡谷、巴黎雄狮凯旋门、梵蒂冈圣彼得大教堂、印度泰姬陵、澳大利亚悉尼歌剧院、意大利比萨斜塔等等。其中，法国埃菲尔铁塔建造比例为1∶3。此外，还有动感刺激的娱乐参与项目、大型广场艺术晚会、异国风情表演、主题文化节庆活动。

☆深圳地铁世界之窗站出入口的造型是一座玻璃金字塔，仿照的是美籍华裔建筑师贝聿铭所设计的巴黎罗浮宫玻璃金字塔。玻璃金字塔上"世界之窗"四个大字为时任国家主席江泽民所题。

☆作为景区活动中心的世界广场，可容纳游客万余人，广场四周耸立着108根不同风格的大石柱和高10米、长近200米的浮雕墙，还有象征世界古老文明发祥地的六座巨门。

深圳市华侨城旅游度假区

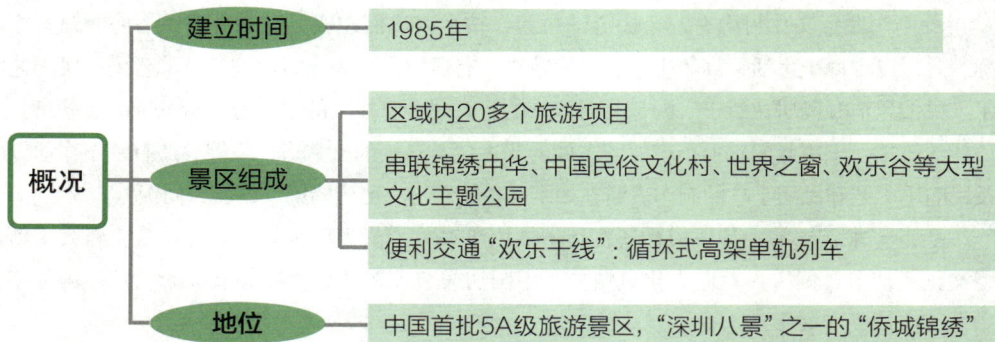

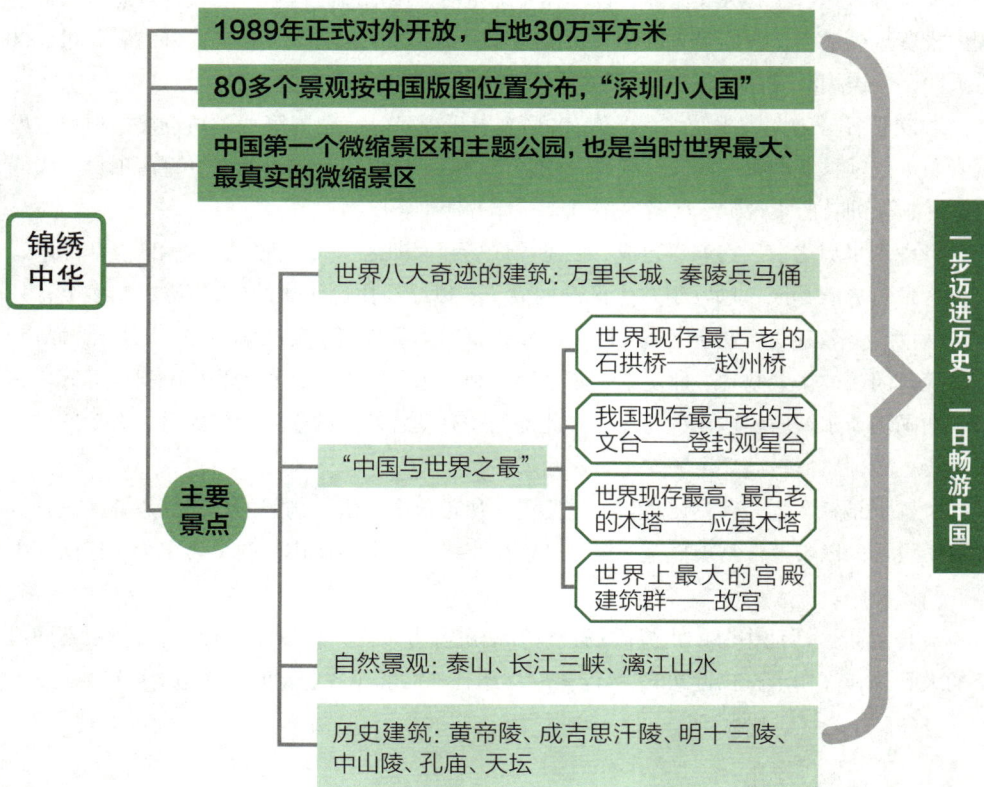

概况
- **建立时间** — 1985年
- **景区组成**
  - 区域内20多个旅游项目
  - 串联锦绣中华、中国民俗文化村、世界之窗、欢乐谷等大型文化主题公园
  - 便利交通"欢乐干线"：循环式高架单轨列车
- **地位** — 中国首批5A级旅游景区，"深圳八景"之一的"侨城锦绣"

锦绣中华
- 1989年正式对外开放，占地30万平方米
- 80多个景观按中国版图位置分布，"深圳小人国"
- 中国第一个微缩景区和主题公园，也是当时世界最大、最真实的微缩景区
- **主要景点**
  - 世界八大奇迹的建筑：万里长城、秦陵兵马俑
  - **"中国与世界之最"**
    - 世界现存最古老的石拱桥——赵州桥
    - 我国现存最古老的天文台——登封观星台
    - 世界现存最高、最古老的木塔——应县木塔
    - 世界上最大的宫殿建筑群——故宫
  - 自然景观：泰山、长江三峡、漓江山水
  - 历史建筑：黄帝陵、成吉思汗陵、明十三陵、中山陵、孔庙、天坛

一步迈进历史，一日畅游中国

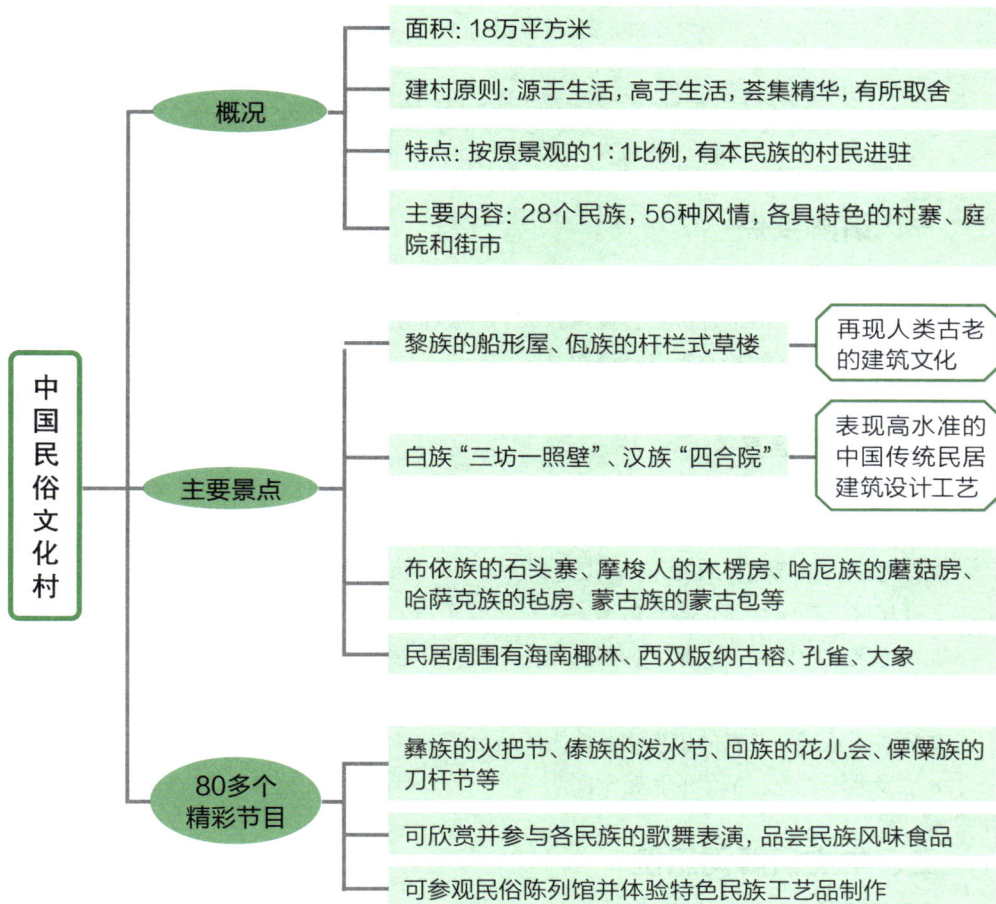

中国民俗文化村

概况
- 面积: 18万平方米
- 建村原则: 源于生活, 高于生活, 荟集精华, 有所取舍
- 特点: 按原景观的1: 1比例, 有本民族的村民进驻
- 主要内容: 28个民族, 56种风情, 各具特色的村寨、庭院和街市

主要景点
- 黎族的船形屋、佤族的杆栏式草楼 —— 再现人类古老的建筑文化
- 白族"三坊一照壁"、汉族"四合院" —— 表现高水准的中国传统民居建筑设计工艺
- 布依族的石头寨、摩梭人的木楞房、哈尼族的蘑菇房、哈萨克族的毡房、蒙古族的蒙古包等
- 民居周围有海南椰林、西双版纳古榕、孔雀、大象

80多个精彩节目
- 彝族的火把节、傣族的泼水节、回族的花儿会、傈僳族的刀杆节等
- 可欣赏并参与各民族的歌舞表演, 品尝民族风味食品
- 可参观民俗陈列馆并体验特色民族工艺品制作

第四节　珠海市海泉湾度假区

一、讲解要点

（一）概述

1.海泉湾度假区的地理位置、规模和八个组成部分。

2.海泉湾度假区的核心卖点：海洋温泉。

3.海泉湾度假区功能齐全、配套完善。

（二）海洋温泉

1.美誉："南海第一泉"。

2.六个特色板块：揽海区、欧风区、东方区、观海区、沐浴娱乐区、"爱琴海"池。

3.揽海区：世界先进的SPA水疗设施。

4.欧风区：死海盐浴、芬兰浴等。

5.东方区：中国的神农泉、韩国的大长今泉、日本的矿砂温泉和石之汤。

6.观海区：古罗马的恺撒泉、土耳其的皇宫浴场、中国的华清池、热海日式露天浴。

7.沐浴娱乐区：儿童的稚趣湾、成人的适意湾、老少咸宜的煮蛋泉。

8."爱琴海"池：情侣的私密空间。

二、中文讲解词示例

【欢迎词】

各位游客朋友们，大家好！欢迎来到全国首个国家旅游休闲度假示范区——海泉湾度假区。

【概述】

海泉湾度假区坐落在珠海市金湾区的海边，占地面积为5.1平方千米。度假区由八个部分组成，包括海洋温泉、海泉湾大酒店、神秘岛、渔人码头、梦幻剧场、健康体检中心、拓展训练营以及运动俱乐部。

海泉湾度假区以海洋温泉为核心，是一个功能齐全、综合配套完善的大型旅游休闲度假区和国际会议中心。

【海洋温泉】

今天主要跟大家介绍海洋温泉。海洋温泉被我国著名医疗矿泉专家陈炎冰教授誉为"南海第一泉"。温泉水温83摄氏度，富含多种有利于人体健康的矿物质和微量元素。

温泉浸泡区包括揽海区、欧风区、东方区、观海区、沐浴娱乐区和"爱琴海"池等六个特色板块。其中揽海区、欧风区、东方区为室内区，观海区、沐浴娱乐区和"爱琴海"

池为室外区。

揽海区是叠水平台水力按摩区，采用世界先进的SPA水疗设施，三级阶梯，2.5米的落差，构成了"三泉叠海"的独特格局。这里有喷射式水力按摩浴池、强力喷水漂浮浴池、冲射按摩浴池、大气泡按摩浴池等多种水疗选择。

欧风区可以体验死海盐池、芬兰浴等。以死海为主题的死海盐池，富含各种矿物质，将死海所出产的矿物盐溶于纯正的海洋温泉水中，从而使温泉水含有更为丰富的矿物质和微量元素，高含盐度还模拟出了死海的水密度，泡温泉的时候人甚至能够浮在水面上，感觉很奇妙。芬兰浴按传统芬兰桑拿房建造，用桦木作炭烧热火山石，使房间的温度高达70摄氏度以上。感觉如何？大家只有试过才知道。

东方区集中了古老神秘的东方国度——中国、日本和韩国的传统温泉项目和发汗设施。这里的神农泉将中草药精华附着于水蒸气中。温泉+中草药，是中国人特有的养生理念。大长今泉属韩国传统的汗蒸幕，能加速新陈代谢，促进微循环。还有日本最独特的温泉浴——矿砂温泉，以石板为床，以热矿砂为被覆盖全身，只露脑袋在外，据说可以让体内的"污气"随热汗蒸发出来。石之汤即日本石板温泉，利用温泉水加热花岗岩石板，您躺在石板上面，便可享受蓝天白云热炕头，好不惬意！

观海区是室外温泉区，集中了几种世界典型的温泉文化。土耳其皇宫浴场按土耳其皇宫浴室建造。古罗马泉大浴场再现了古罗马恺撒大帝所建造的阿拉里帕帕大浴场的奢华场景。华清池则以中国唐代风格为主题设计，有"莲花池"和"海棠池"，再现了当年杨贵妃"春寒水暖洗凝脂"的场景。热海日式露天浴选取了日本最具代表性的温泉——草津温泉田为原型，充满浓郁的日式风情。

沐浴娱乐区是把洗浴和游乐结合的天堂。在游乐中洗浴，在洗浴中游乐。这里的溶洞温泉造型别致，温泉瀑布挂在溶洞温泉的洞口，极具吸引力，游客如置身于溶洞之中。稚趣湾是儿童戏水乐园，旁边神秘的古代帆船带给小朋友无限的遐想空间。而适意湾是成人戏水游泳的地方，冬暖夏凉，还有水上篮球等设施。您吃过"温泉蛋"吗？这里的煮蛋泉可以让您品尝独特的温泉蛋。83摄氏度的热水，10分钟便可把鸡蛋煮熟，而且煮出来的温泉蛋是咸的，蛋白像果冻，别有风味。

爱琴海是希腊著名的蜜月胜地，海洋温泉的"爱琴海"是专门为情侣设计的九个大小不等的温泉池。情侣们可以在这里尽享伊甸园般的私密空间。"缘分的天空，情定爱琴海。"这里不仅让您尽情享受着洗浴的快乐，还有望海吧、听海吧、品海吧等露天休息室供您消遣放松。

【结束语】

我的导览到此结束，感谢大家的聆听！剩下的时间留给大家亲自体验泡温泉的快乐。祝大家玩得开心愉快！

三、英文讲解词示例

Haiquan Bay Resort in Zhuhai

Dear guests! Welcome to Haiquan Bay Resort in Zhuhai!

Located in Jinwan District in Zhuhai City, Haiquan Bay Resort is facing the beautiful South China Sea. It has an area of 5.1 square kilometers.

With ocean hot spring as its key highlight, Haiquan Bay Resort is a large tourism resort and international conference hall with full-fledged facilities.

Today, I would like to introduce the ocean hot spring. Ocean hot spring is extolled as the "No.1 Spring in South China Sea" by Professor Chen Yanbing, a renowned medical spring expert in China. At a temperature of 83℃, hot spring water here contains multiple minerals and micro elements that are beneficial to human bodies.

Bath area has 6 areas, including Cascading Ocean Area, European Style Area, Oriental Style Area, Ocean Viewing Area, Bath Entertainment Area and Aegean Sea Area.

The Cascading Ocean Area is a cascading platform with the function of hydraulic massage. Equipped with advanced SPA facilities in the world, the three-layered platform has the drop height of 2.5 meters and forms a unique picture of "three hot springs constitute a sea". This area offers various choices such as spray hydraulic massage bath pool, strong spray floating bath pool, impingement massage bath pool, bubble massage pool and so on.

In the European Style Area, you can enjoy the Dead Sea Salt Pool and Finnish Hot Spring. With the Dead Sea as the theme, the Dead Sea Salt Pool contains a lot of minerals. By injecting mineral salt imported from the Dead Sea into pure ocean hot spring, the hot spring water contains rich and diversified minerals and micro elements. The high salinity also simulates the water density of the Dead Sea, when taking a hot spring bath, it is definitely a wonderful feeling to float on the water. The Finnish Hot Spring is built according to traditional Finnish sauna room. Birch branches are burnt to warm volcanic rock so the room can reach the temperature of over 70℃. How do you feel? You can never tell the feelings until you really have a try.

In the Oriental Style Area, visitors can enjoy traditional hot spring and diaphoresis programs from the orient such as China, Japan and Korea. In the Shennong Hot Spring, essence of traditional Chinese herbs are mixed with vapour. It is our unique Chinese health preserving philosophy to combine hot spring with traditional Chinese herbs. The Dae Jang Geum Bath is traditional "hanjeungmak" from Korea. The unique way of sweating can facilitate metabolism and micro circulation of human bodies. You can also enjoy the Ore Hot Spring, a unique Japanese hot spring. Lying on stone panels, visitors have their bodies, except their heads, covered in hot ore sand. It is said that such method can detox the bodies by sweating. The Stone Hot Spring, or called "Stone Panel Hot Spring", uses hot spring water to heat granite panels. It feels so good to comfortably lie on warm panels and look at sky and clouds.

The Sea Viewing Area is an outdoor bath which shows various hot spring cultures at the same time. The Turkey Royal Palace Hot Spring, according to its name, is a reproduction of bath in Turkish Royal Palace. The Caesar Hot Spring reproduces the scene of Thermae Agrippae built by the Emperor Caesar in ancient Rome. The Huaqing Hot Spring is designed and built with a style of the Tang Dynasty in ancient China. Comprised of Lotus Pool and Asiatic Apple Pool, it reminds people of a poem describing Lady Yang, one of the four beauties in ancient China, taking a bath in Huaqing Pool: "Wash jade-like skin with hot spring in chilly season." The Japanese Atami Outdoor Hot Spring replicates Kusatsu Onsen, the most representative hot spring in Japan. It is not surprising to see rich Japanese flavor here.

The Bath Entertainment Area is a paradise for both bathing and entertainment. Visitors can take a bath while enjoying a lot of fun here. The whole venue looks like a karst cave, which is unique and novel. One can see a hot spring cascade at the entry of the cave, which is appealing and creates an immersive feeling. The Happy Childhood Bay is a water park for kids. Mystic ancient sailboat encourages children to have imagination. The Leisure Bay is a water park for adults. It is warm in winter and cool in summer. Visitors can also play water basketball here. Have you ever tasted "hot spring eggs"? The Egg Boiling Hot Spring allows you to taste unique-flavored "hot spring eggs". 83℃ boiling water can cook an egg thoroughly in just 10 minutes. The salty egg has jelly-like egg white, which is divine!

In Greek, Aegean Sea is a famous tourist destination for honeymoon. The Aegean Sea Area, with 9 hot springs in different sizes, is specifically designed for lovers. They can enjoy private space in this paradise. "Marriage is made in heaven; love is witnessed in Aegean Sea." In this area, you can not only fully enjoy the pleasure of bathing, but also relax in several outdoor common rooms such as the Sea Viewing Bar, Sea Listening Bar and Sea Appreciation Bar.

That's the end of my tour guide commentary. Thank you for listening! Now it's time for you to enjoy hot springs here! Have fun!

四、综合知识

☆2007年，海泉湾度假区被国家旅游局授予全国首个"国家旅游休闲度假示范区"称号。2015年7月，海泉湾海洋温泉荣获五星级温泉美誉。

☆海泉湾度假区以海洋温泉为核心，由海洋温泉、海泉湾大酒店、神秘岛主题乐园、渔人码头、梦幻剧场、健康体检中心、拓展训练营以及运动俱乐部等组成，是一个功能齐全、综合配套完善的大型旅游休闲度假区和国际会议中心。

☆海洋温泉水质清澈，出水口水温常年保持在78~83℃，泉井自喷高达11米，是罕见的优质海底温泉，属含硅酸和氡的弱浓度氯化钠泉，富含30多种对人体有益的微量元素和矿物质，具有良好的纤体、美肤、活血等保健功效，被我国著名医疗矿泉专家陈炎冰教授誉为"南海第一泉"。

☆海洋温泉中心依托天然海洋温泉而建，毗邻大海。它由分布在室内外的80多个形状不一、功能各异的温泉池和10多种发汗设施组成。囊括了古今中外丰富多彩的温泉沐浴文化。

☆揽海区采用世界先进的SPA水疗设施，三级阶梯以及2.5米的落差，构成了"三泉叠海"的独特格局。有喷射式水力按摩浴池、强力喷水漂浮浴池、冲射按摩浴池、大气泡按摩浴池等多种水疗选择。欧风区有死海盐池、芬兰浴。东方区有神农泉、大长今泉、矿砂温泉等，还有日本石板温泉"石之汤"。

☆观海区位于室外温泉区，有古罗马的恺撒泉、土耳其皇宫浴场、热海日式露天浴、唐风华清池等。沐浴娱乐区有溶洞温泉、沙滩温泉、"爱琴海"温泉池等，游客还可以在煮蛋泉品尝温泉蛋。煮蛋泉水温为83℃，10分钟便可把鸡蛋煮熟。

☆海洋园林温泉区有各类中草药、精油、牛奶、咖啡等风格各异的温泉沐浴方式，游客能获得更丰富的温泉沐浴体验。

珠海市海泉湾度假区

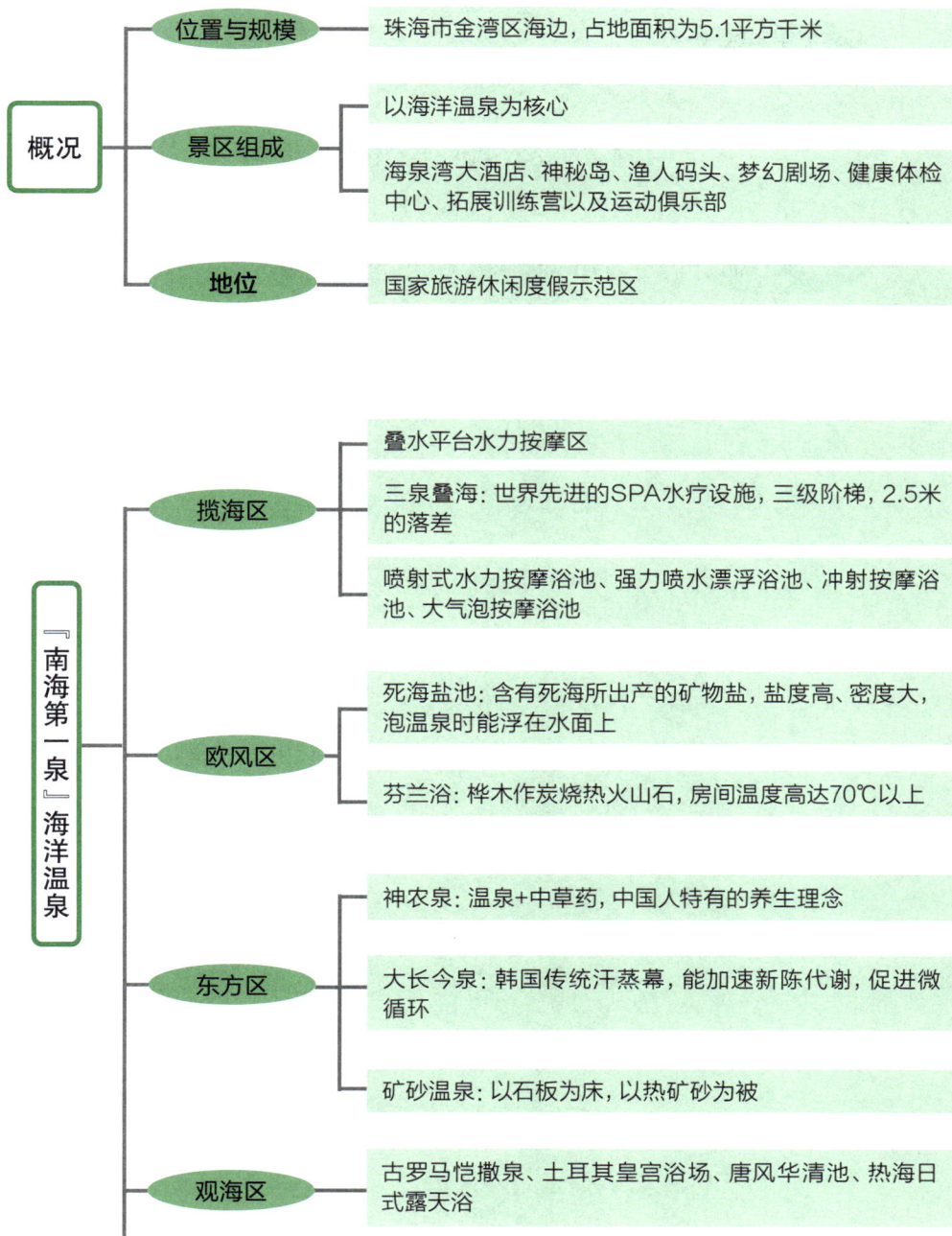

概况
- **位置与规模** —— 珠海市金湾区海边，占地面积为5.1平方千米
- **景区组成**
  - 以海洋温泉为核心
  - 海泉湾大酒店、神秘岛、渔人码头、梦幻剧场、健康体检中心、拓展训练营以及运动俱乐部
- **地位** —— 国家旅游休闲度假示范区

『南海第一泉』海洋温泉
- **揽海区**
  - 叠水平台水力按摩区
  - 三泉叠海：世界先进的SPA水疗设施，三级阶梯，2.5米的落差
  - 喷射式水力按摩浴池、强力喷水漂浮浴池、冲射按摩浴池、大气泡按摩浴池
- **欧风区**
  - 死海盐池：含有死海所出产的矿物盐，盐度高、密度大，泡温泉时能浮在水面上
  - 芬兰浴：桦木作炭烧热火山石，房间温度高达70℃以上
- **东方区**
  - 神农泉：温泉+中草药，中国人特有的养生理念
  - 大长今泉：韩国传统汗蒸幕，能加速新陈代谢，促进微循环
  - 矿砂温泉：以石板为床，以热矿砂为被
- **观海区** —— 古罗马恺撒泉、土耳其皇宫浴场、唐风华清池、热海日式露天浴

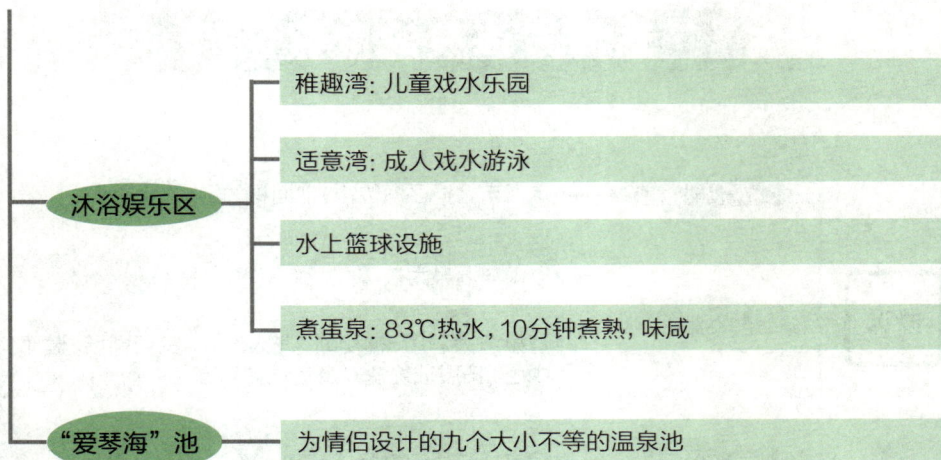

沐浴娱乐区

稚趣湾：儿童戏水乐园

适意湾：成人戏水游泳

水上篮球设施

煮蛋泉：83℃热水，10分钟煮熟，味咸

"爱琴海"池 —— 为情侣设计的九个大小不等的温泉池

第五节　佛山市西樵山景区

一、讲解要点

（一）概述

1.西樵山的地理位置和荣誉。

2.西樵山的成因。

3.西樵山名称的由来。

4.西樵山的特点及主要景区。

（二）白云洞景区

1.白云洞的地理位置及名称由来。

2.奎光塔：白云洞的标志性建筑。

3.白云古寺、飞来塔、三湖书院。

4.云泉仙馆、大云泉。

二、中文讲解词示例

【欢迎词】

各位游客，大家好！欢迎来到西樵山参观游览。

【概述】

西樵山位于佛山市南海区西南部，地处珠江三角洲的中心。山周近似圆形，直径约4千米，占地面积约14平方千米。主峰为大科峰，海拔344米。西樵山是广东四大名山之一，同时还集国家5A级旅游景区、国家地质公园、国家森林公园、国家重点风景名胜区等桂冠于一身。*速记 ①直4（直径），面14（面积），高344（海拔高）；涉及数据，要么不讲，讲就不能错。②三中心、四大、5A、地质、森林、风景。

西樵山是一座死火山。有人也许要问了，为什么在珠江三角洲这么一大块平原上，单单这里有一座死火山呢？这还得要从4500万年前说起，那时候珠江三角洲还是个古海湾，因一次海底火山爆发，喷出大量岩浆，在海里凝结，成为一个锥状的山体。后来又出现了几次岩浆喷发，在大锥体上架叠了许多小锥体，于是就形成了峰峦簇拥、状若莲花的西樵山。

西樵山和罗浮山共享"南粤名山数二樵"之美誉。西樵山最早叫锦石山，是因为岩浆冷却形成的山石颜色众多，"色灿如锦"而得名。那为什么后来又叫西樵山呢？"樵"是打柴的意思，传说古时候广州人烧的柴火主要来自罗浮山和锦石山，罗浮山在广州东面，称为"东樵"，锦石山位于广州西面，就叫作"西樵"。

西樵山除了叫锦石山之外，还有两个别称。其一是因晚唐诗人曹松曾隐居西樵山，他教山民开荒种茶，种出来的云雾茶成为本地特产，故西樵山又称"茶山"；其二是因明清两代常有名士在山中设书院，讲学论道，探求心性，西樵山又被人们称为"理学名山"。

西樵山风景资源非常丰富，最大的特点是"山里有湖，湖里有山，水在山中，山在水中"。号称有72峰、48洞、28瀑布、208泉、东西2湖。主要有"白天九石翠碧黄"七个景区，分别为白云洞、天湖公园、九龙岩、石燕岩、翠岩、碧玉洞、黄飞鸿狮艺武术馆。

【白云洞】

各位游客，现在我们来到的是白云洞景区。白云洞位于西樵山西北麓。说它是洞，其实是由长庚、白云、幡子三座山峰环抱而成的山谷，划分为三个洞天，命名为24景。明嘉靖年间，西樵学子何亮在这里搭建书屋读书，号称"白云先生"，后人就以"白云"为洞名。此后名流汇聚于此，栽花植树，筑舍建院，现在白云洞已经成为佛、道、儒三教共处的福地。*速记 游览顺序：塔→寺→塔→院→仙→泉。

【奎光塔】

大家现在看到的这座三层的塔，叫作奎光塔。塔高15米，因其外形看上去好像一支笔尾向下、笔尖向上的毛笔，所以俗称"文笔塔"。据说是科举时代为了祈求文运亨通、赴考高中而建。该塔端庄肃穆，是白云洞的标志性建筑。

【白云古寺】

继续往前，我们来到的便是白云古寺，该寺建于明代，距今已有400多年的历史。白云寺揽山面湖，在湖边巨石上矗立的这座塔叫作飞来塔，塔高7层。塔后面的是三湖书院，是康有为先生青年时期读书的地方。我们现在见到的是重建后的三湖书院，当年康有为就是在这里探求救国救民的真理，走出三湖书院，发动了轰轰烈烈的戊戌变法，可以说这里是戊戌变法的摇篮。大家请看书院的门匾，是民族英雄林则徐亲笔题写的。

【云泉仙馆】

沿着通道拾级而上，现在大家见到的这座庄严肃穆的古庙堂式建筑就是云泉仙馆，这里是供奉八仙之一吕洞宾的庙宇。馆门上的石匾题有"云泉仙馆"四个字。这四个字是由清朝的耆英所题写的，有细心的游客发现了"仙"字的中间那一竖歪向了一边，大家知道为什么吗？有人说是因为耆英签定了中国近代史上第一个不平等条约——《南京条约》，这丧权辱国的条约，使清朝江山摇摇欲坠，所以中间这一竖歪向了一边。

【大云泉】

最后我们来到飞流千尺瀑布大云泉，曾被列为清代"羊城八景"之一。泉水从西天湖坝底流出，从洗心石仰头观望，飞泻的瀑布被风吹得如烟如雾如尘，让人心旷神怡。

据说康有为年轻的时候曾经盘坐在洗心石上，用棉花塞住耳朵，隔绝水声，专心攻读。

【结束语】

各位游客，秀丽清幽的西樵山景区的游览到此结束了，感谢大家的支持和配合，祝大家玩得开心，再见。

三、英文讲解词示例

Foshan Xiqiao Mountain Scenic Area

Dear visitors, welcome to Xiqiao Mountain.

Located in southwestern Nanhai District of Foshan, Xiqiao Mountain is in the center of the Pearl River Delta. If you have a bird's eye view of Xiqiao Mountain, you will see the shape of the mountain is like a circle. It is 4 km in diameter, covering an area of 14 square kilometers. The main peak is Dake Peak which is 344 meters high. As one of the "Four Famous Mountains in Guangdong", Xiqiao Mountain also earns reputation of the "National 5A Scenic Area", "National Geopark", "National Forest Park" and "National Park of China".

Xiqiao Mountain is an extinct volcano. Some of you might wonder why a extinct volcano stands on the vast plain of the Pearl River Delta Region. 45 million years ago, the Pearl River Delta Region was an ocean bay. Then a submarine volcano erupted and the magma froze under the sea and formed a cone-shape massif. After that, there were more volcano eruptions, which added many smaller coned hills on it. That's how the Xiqiao Mountain had taken its lotus-like shape.

Xiqiao and Luofu are two famous mountains in Guangdong. In the past, Xiqiao Mountain was called "Jinshi Mountain" because the color of pozzolan stone is as bright as brocade. "Jin" in Chinese means "brocade". Then why changed the name to "Xiqiao"? Because "Qiao" in Chinese means "collecting firewood". It is said that in ancient times, firewood in Guangzhou mostly came from Luofu Mountain and Jinshi Mountain. The former one was to the east of Guangzhou and was called "Dongqiao". "Dong" means "east". The latter one was to the west of the city and was called "Xiqiao". "Xi" means "west" in Chinese.

In addition to "Jinshi Mountain", Xiqiao Mountain was also called the "Tea Mountain" because Cao Song, a poet in the Tang Dynasty lived here and taught locals to reclaim wasteland and grow Yunwu Tea. The tea has become a special local product in Xiqiao Mountain. Another name was the "Mountain of Neo-Confucianism" because many famous scholars in the Ming Dynasty and Qing Dynasty came here and set up academies in Xiqiao Mountain, lecturing on Neo-Confucianism and debating philosophies.

Xiqiao Mountain Scenic Area has rich tourism resources. Here, hills surround lakes and the lakes mirror the hills. Waters and mountains add poetic beauty to each other. There are 72 peaks, 48 caves, 28 waterfalls, 208 springs and two lakes. There are 7 major scenic spots, including Baiyun Cave, Tianhu Park, the Nine Dragon Rock, the Stone Swallow Rock, the Green Rock, the Jade Cave and the Fei Fong Wong Lion Dance Martial Arts Hall.

Dear guests, now we are in Baiyun Cave Scenic Spot which is located at the northwest of

Xiqiao Mountain. It was built during Emperor Jiajing's reign in the 16th century. It was called "cave", but actually it is a cave-like valley surrounded by three peaks: Changgeng Peak, Baiyun Peak and Fanzi Peak. The whole place is divided into three parts with 24 scenic spots. During Emperor Jiajing's reign, a scholar called He Liang built a cottage and studied here. Thus he had another name "Mr.Baiyun" and later generations named the place after him. Then it attracted many famous scholars who build cottages and lived a simple life here. Now it has become a blessed place where Buddhism, Taoism and Confucianism coexist.

The three-layered building in front of you is Kuiguang Tower. Standing 15 meters tall, it looks like a brush pen with its tip pointing skyward. So we also call it "Wenbi Tower" which means Pen Tower. In the feudal society, the tower was built for scholars to pray for better luck and high score in the imperial exams so that they can become government officials. The solemn and grand tower is an iconic building in Baiyun Cave.

Moving forward and we are now at Baiyun Ancient Temple. Built in the Ming Dynasty, it has a history of over 400 years. The temple sits on a mountain and faces a lake. Feilai Pagoda is a 7-storied building standing on a huge rock by the lake. Behind it stands Sanhu Academy. It was here that young Kang Youwei studied and sought the truth of saving the country and its people. After leaving Sanhu Academy, he launched the famous Hundred Days' Reform. So it is fair to say Sanhu Academy is the cradle of Hundred Days' Reform. Look at the plaque of this academy, the Chinese characters on it were written by Lin Zexu who is a well-known national hero in China.

Climbing the steps along the passageway and you will see Yunquan Pavilion. It is a shrine for worshiping Lv Dongbin, one of the legendary Eight Immortals in China. The name on of the Pavilion was inscribed by Qi Ying, a A Qing Dynasty government official. Some visitors would find that the downward stroke in the middle of the character "Xian" is tilted. Do you know why? People guess the reason is that Qi Ying signed the *Treaty of Nanjing*. It was the first unequal treaty in the history of contemporary China. It was a humiliating treaty that compromised national sovereignty and left the Qing Dynasty's rule in jeopardy, the vertical stroke as a result in the middle of the character "Xian" slanted to one side.

In the end, we came to Dayun Spring. In the Qing Dynasty, the waterfall which is over a thousand feet high used to be one of the eight famous scenic spots of Guangzhou. Spring water comes out from the bottom of Tianhu Dam. Standing on the Xixin Stone and looking up, descending water flying in the wind looks like smoke, mist or dust, which brings a sense of tranquility and joy to people.

It is said that when Kang Youwei was young, he used to sit on the Xixin Stone and read. In order to concentrate on his reading, he often put cotton in his ears to block out the water sound.

So dear visitors, that's the end of our tour in picturesque Xiqiao Mountain. Thank you for your support and cooperation. Have fun and see you.

四、综合知识

☆广东有"南粤名山数二樵"的说法，"二樵"指的是"东樵"罗浮山，"西樵"西樵山。"樵"是打柴的意思。

☆唐代诗人曹松曾躬耕隐居于西樵山。他发现这里的土壤、水质、气候都非常适合茶树的生长，于是就引进优质茶种，教山民种植、采摘、焙制，生产的云雾茶（又名苦丁茶）远近闻名，西樵山于是有了"茶山"之名。

☆西樵山本来的名字叫锦石山，因为峰石灿烂如锦而得名。山石种类繁多，有十多种颜色，有灰色、灰绿色、紫色、粉红色、灰黄色的粗面岩，灰白色、白色的火山角砾岩，黑色、灰黑色的燧石，等等，令人眼花缭乱。其中燧石、玛瑙石、霏细岩等石头质地坚硬、可塑性强，是制造石器的优良石料。

☆西樵山是一座古死火山，是4500万—5100万年前白垩纪中后期多次火山喷发形成的，是珠三角地区保存得较为完整的地质遗址，也是研究华南第三纪火山活动和火山地貌的理想场所。

☆1958年，著名考古学家贾兰坡等人发现西樵山以细石器和双肩石器为特征的史前人类活动古遗址，认为是我国华南史前时期最大的石器制造场。火山喷出的大量岩浆冷却后形成西樵山最早的山体，而构成山体的岩石具有细密结构，使其在制作工具时容易成型，便于控制。

☆经考古专家初步发现，西樵山石燕岩景区的水下遗址面积达数十万平方米，是迄今发现的国内最大、最完整、最壮观的水下古代生产遗迹，具有重要的历史科考价值。

☆2024年6月27日，广东文物考古研究院、南海博物馆发布最新研究成果：确认西樵山平面岗遗址包含新石器时代和旧石器时代两个时期的遗存，是广佛地区目前发现的年代最早的人类遗存，将西樵山人类活动足迹上溯至4万年前。

☆明代，湛若水等在西樵山先后创建四大书院——大科书院（湛若水）、石泉书院（方献夫）、四峰书院（霍韬陆）、云谷书院（湛若水），其中名声最大、开建最早的是大科书院，当时几乎能与湖南岳麓书院、江西白鹿书院媲美。大批文人学子隐居西樵，探求理学，锤炼心性，使西樵山获得了"南粤理学名山"的雅号。如今仅四峰书院留有遗址。

☆清代，西樵人岑怀瑾在西樵山白云洞创建三湖书院。书院牌匾"三湖书院"四个大字出自清代名臣林则徐之手。康有为曾求学于三湖书院，自号"西樵山人"。他在西樵山求学两年，广泛涉猎各家经典，探寻维新强国之道，为日后推动戊戌变法奠定了坚实的思想基础。因此，三湖书院被誉为戊戌变法的摇篮。

☆西樵山是著名的南拳、南狮文化发源地。1847年，一代武林宗师黄飞鸿出生在西樵山下禄舟村，村中如今兴建有黄飞鸿狮艺武术馆。从2000年起，西樵山每年都会举办全国南北狮王争霸赛和世界华人狮王争霸赛。2005年，西樵镇被国家体育总局授予"中国龙狮名镇"称号。

☆西樵山春山杜鹃映红，漫山如披锦绣，秋山层林尽染，丹桂飘香，黄菊遍野，因此西樵山又称花山，据说南越王赵佗就常于西樵山春游观花。

☆在石燕岩古采石场遗址不远处，有一块"回樵"石。据说，西汉初年，皇帝两次派重臣陆贾说服赵佗归汉，赵佗和陆贾两次同赴西樵山，谈判顺利，赵佗两次归汉。"回樵"由此成为千年佳话，"回樵"一词也成了好运的象征。

☆桑园围，又称"桑园围水利设施"，位于西樵山南麓，开启了珠江三角洲地区大规模基围农耕开发的历史，是桑基鱼塘生产方式的发端。2020年，桑园围入选第七批世界灌溉工程遗产，与四川都江堰、陕西郑国渠、广西灵渠等齐名。

☆白云洞之"洞"，其实是由长庚、白云、华盖三座山峰环抱而成的一个深谷。明代，西樵学子何亮在此筑台营室，养性读书，自号"白云先生"，洞便由此得名。此后，白云洞逐渐成为儒、释、道潜修、传教、授业的共享福地。

☆白云洞景区的大门两侧，有双峰对峙如门。左为天镇峰，有巨石似一位道士；右为吉水峰，有巨石如一个和尚。因此，白云洞这一道景观被叫作"僧道守云门"。

☆奎光楼，楼高15米，方形三层，是科举时代学子们为祈求文运亨通、赴考高中而建。正面门额题写"万里云衢"，背面门额则是"凤翔千仞"四字。

☆云泉仙馆是一座庄严肃穆的古道观，供奉八仙之一的吕洞宾。馆门匾额"云泉仙馆"为清代两广总督耆英所书。云泉仙馆原名为"攻玉楼"，因其为南海石岗乡李攻玉所建。每当夏秋之际，蝉鸣清脆，因而又有"攻玉听蝉"之美景。

☆大云泉位于白云洞中，又名"飞流千尺"瀑布，是清代"羊城八景"之一。相传，康有为在此游学时，曾盘坐洗心石上，以棉团塞耳，潜心苦读。

佛山市西樵山景区

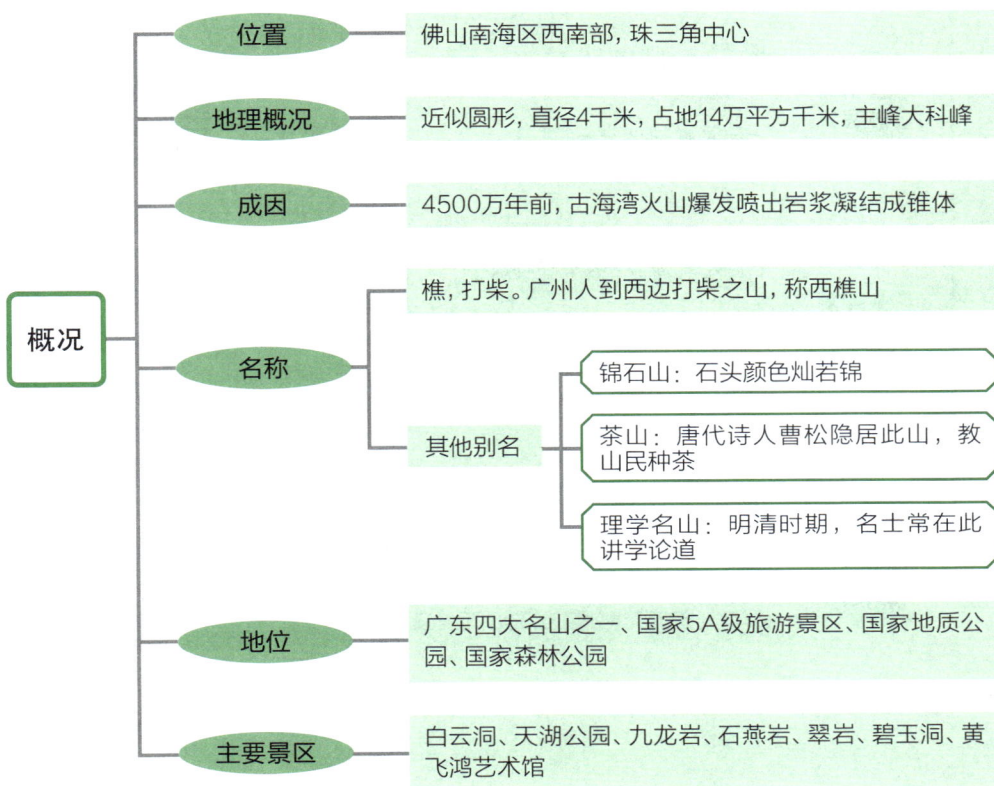

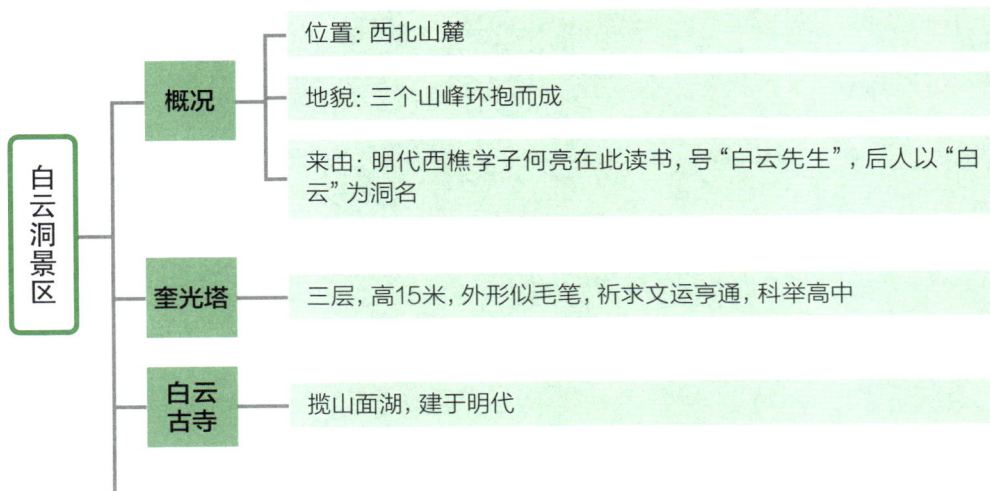

概况

- **位置** —— 佛山南海区西南部，珠三角中心

- **地理概况** —— 近似圆形，直径4千米，占地14万平方千米，主峰大科峰

- **成因** —— 4500万年前，古海湾火山爆发喷出岩浆凝结成锥体

- **名称**
  - 樵，打柴。广州人到西边打柴之山，称西樵山
  - **其他别名**
    - 锦石山：石头颜色灿若锦
    - 茶山：唐代诗人曹松隐居此山，教山民种茶
    - 理学名山：明清时期，名士常在此讲学论道

- **地位** —— 广东四大名山之一、国家5A级旅游景区、国家地质公园、国家森林公园

- **主要景区** —— 白云洞、天湖公园、九龙岩、石燕岩、翠岩、碧玉洞、黄飞鸿艺术馆

白云洞景区

- **概况**
  - 位置：西北山麓
  - 地貌：三个山峰环抱而成
  - 来由：明代西樵学子何亮在此读书，号"白云先生"，后人以"白云"为洞名

- **奎光塔** —— 三层，高15米，外形似毛笔，祈求文运亨通，科举高中

- **白云古寺** —— 揽山面湖，建于明代

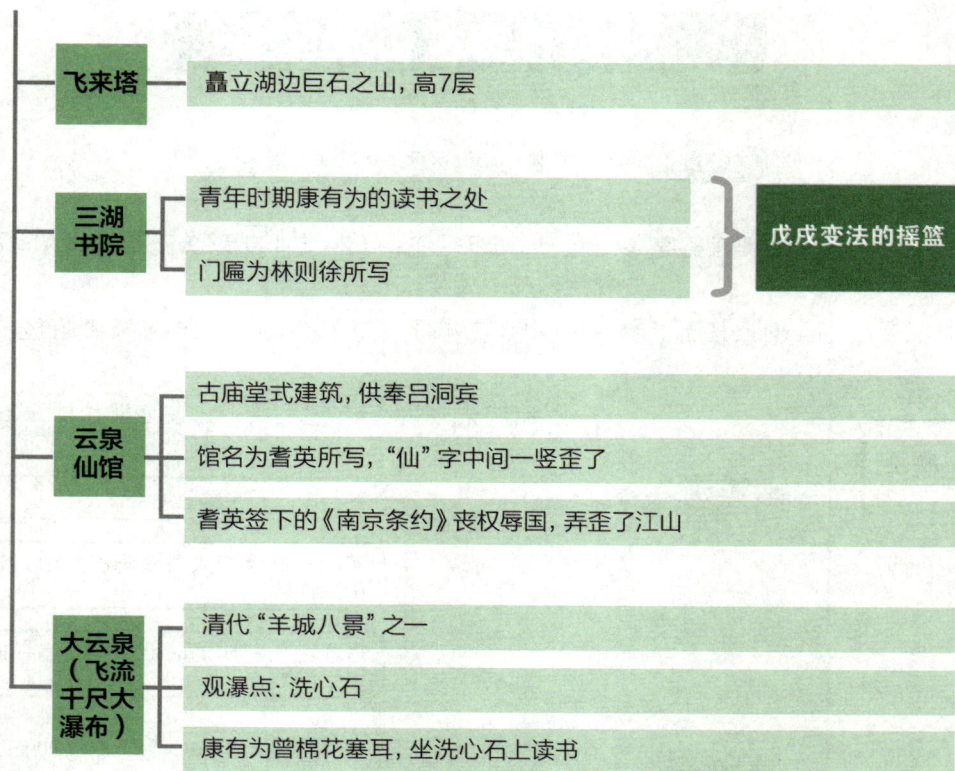

飞来塔	矗立湖边巨石之山，高7层
三湖书院	青年时期康有为的读书之处
	门匾为林则徐所写
云泉仙馆	古庙堂式建筑，供奉吕洞宾
	馆名为耆英所写，"仙"字中间一竖歪了
	耆英签下的《南京条约》丧权辱国，弄歪了江山
大云泉（飞流千尺大瀑布）	清代"羊城八景"之一
	观瀑点：洗心石
	康有为曾棉花塞耳，坐洗心石上读书

戊戌变法的摇篮（三湖书院）

第六节 韶关市丹霞山景区

一、讲解要点

（一）概述

1.丹霞山以及丹霞地貌的得名由来。

2.丹霞山的位置、美誉和地位。

3.丹霞山景区的构成。

（二）长老峰

1.长老峰的下中上三层景观简介。

2.介绍下层景观，包括梦觉关、"幽洞通天"、"一线天"、锦岩等。

3.介绍中层景观，包括别传寺、鸳鸯树、丹梯铁索等。

4.介绍上层景观观日亭。

二、中文讲解词示例

【欢迎词】

各位游客，大家好！欢迎来到丹霞山参观游览。

【概述】

丹霞山的得名源于古人称赞这里"色如渥丹，灿若明霞"，因其独特的红色砂砾岩形成丹霞地貌。那什么叫"丹霞地貌"呢？早在20世纪30年代，中科院院士、中山大学教授陈国达在对丹霞山及华南地区的红石山做了深入研究后，就以面积最大、发育最典型、类型最齐全、风景最优美的韶关丹霞山作为"丹霞地貌"的命名地。

丹霞地貌的形成是多种地质作用共同作用的结果，最主要的是长期的风化作用，最终形成了如今我们看到的千奇百怪、形态各异的方山、石墙、石峰、石柱等独特形态。

全球丹霞地貌以中国分布最广，而其中最有名的当属丹霞山了，它位于广东韶关仁化县，距韶关市区45千米，总面积292平方千米，最高峰巴寨海拔619.2米。它以"赤壁丹崖"而扬名四海，被誉为"中国的红石公园"，也是"广东四大名山"之首。

丹霞山景区从1980年起对外旅游开放。1988年经国务院批准为国家级风景名胜区；2004年、2010年分别被联合国教科文组织评为世界地质公园、世界自然遗产；2011年被评为国家5A级旅游景区。

丹霞山景区目前已开发的游览区主要是北部的丹霞山景区和西部的巴寨景区，包括长老峰游览区、阳元山游览区、翔龙湖—卧龙岗游览区和锦江长廊游览区。

【长老峰】

各位游客，我们今天要游览的是长老峰，分上中下三层景观：我们先前往下层游览锦石岩石窟，它是历史悠久的佛教道场，也是丹霞山重要地质科考线路。然后我们会到达中层，参观别传寺、鸳鸯树、丹梯铁索；最后在上层的山顶观日亭观云海、看日出、赏晚霞，感受"一览众山小"的气概。在南面山麓是阴元石、翔龙湖和仙居岩道观。*速记 游览顺序：下→中→上。

【下层：梦觉关、"幽洞通天"、"一线天"、锦岩】

各位游客，现在我们已经来到了下层景观锦石岩，主要景点有梦觉关、幽洞通天、一线天、锦岩等。

梦觉关是一个大型蜂窝状风化洞穴，岩穴长6米，进深2.5米，高2米。宋代，法云居士游览锦石岩时，发现了这处岩洞，说它形状奇特，环境清幽，犹如天然形成的一座关房，是个修炼的好地方。他恋恋不舍，感叹说："半生奔波如梦幻，今日方觉此清虚！"后人于是把这个岩洞称为"梦觉关"。

前面就是"幽洞通天"，这是一个自然风化的岩洞。现在大家跟着我穿洞而过，这里就是我国已发现的最长、最高、最壮观的"一线天"，峡长200多米，高70多米，最窄处仅有70厘米。继续往前走过"浸碧浮金""喷玉泉"，就进入了锦岩。

锦岩由几个天然洞穴相连，分别建有七佛殿、观音殿、大雄宝殿等，其中观音殿岩洞最大，洞内塑有观音32相，可容纳数百善信同时参拜。

各位游客，我们现在抬头看一下大雄宝殿的崖壁，那里有被称为丹霞十二景之"片鳞秋月"的"龙鳞"，它春天的时候是嫩绿色的，夏天深绿，秋天黄绿，冬天褐黄。这是为什么呢？原来是由于因风化而造成的蜂窝状岩壁上，生长着蓝藻等生物，吸水性很强。天气潮湿时，吸水越多，呈现的颜色越深绿；到干旱季节，吸到的水分极少，就呈现淡淡的褐黄色，因此有"变色龙"之称。

接下来我们出来凭栏欣赏一下丹霞山的摩崖石刻，眼前的"锦岩"二字为宋朝赵汝耒所题写，也是丹霞山现存最早的摩崖石刻。丹霞山景区的摩崖石刻于2013年被列为全国点文物保护单位。

接下来请大家跟随我，走捷径登上中层风景区。

【中层：别传寺、鸳鸯树、丹梯铁索】

我们先游览岭南十大名刹之一的别传寺。别传寺建于清康熙元年，因禅宗"不立文字，心印别传"而得名。

这棵就是鸳鸯树了，它其实是由百日青和笔管榕两棵不同科属的树缠绕而成。"在天愿作比翼鸟，在地愿为连理枝"，据说相爱的人们手牵手，绕树三周，可缘定三生，有情人终成眷属！

我们在御风亭休息一会，接下来挑战"宜若登天"的"丹梯铁索"，有句话叫："没有爬过丹梯铁索，等于没来丹霞山；不登长老峰，旅游一场空。"大家务必都要尝试下哦！大家看，"宜若登天"的"宜"字少了一点，是不是写错了？其实是作者别出心裁，取其"差一点可登天"之意，暗寓其险犹如登天。

【上层：观日亭】

各位游客，现在我们登上天梯，终于来到了上层风景区观日亭。观日亭是绝佳的观景点，早晨可看日出，傍晚可赏晚霞。来来来，我们先往东面看看，那座就是著名的僧帽峰了，是不是非常形似？东面还有望郎归、宝塔峰、蜡烛峰；南面有金龟回头、骆驼峰、韶石山群峰；西面有姐妹峰、玉壶峰、巴寨、朝天龙、送子观音等远景；北面有睡美人、群象出山。山顶还可游览雪岩、海螺峰、宝珠峰、虹桥拥翠、舵石朝曦等景观。

【结束语】

我的讲解到此结束，但大家美好的丹霞山之旅才刚刚开始，祝大家旅途愉快！谢谢大家！

三、英文讲解词示例

Danxia Mountain Scenic Area in Shaoguan

Dear visitors, welcome to Danxia Mountain.

Our ancestors once praised that the color of Danxia Mountain is like red lily, bright as sunset glow. That's how the mountain got its name. In Chinese, "Dan" means "red color" and "Xia" means "sunset glow". Unique red glutenite form Danxia landscape. What is "Danxia"? Back to the 1930s, Chen Guoda, an academician of the Chinese Academy of Sciences and a professor of Sun Yat-sen University carried out an in-depth research of redstone mountains in Danxia Mountain and south China region. He named such topographical condition after Danxia Mountain, China's largest redstone area with the most typical topographical development, complete geological types and the best scenery.

Danxia landscape is the result of multiple geological processes, with long-term weathering as its main reason. That's why we can see numerous grotesque stones and peaks here.

China has the largest area of Danxia landscape. And the most famous one is Danxia Mountain. Located in Renhua County of Shaoguan, it is 45km away from urban areas and covers an area of 292 square kilometers. Bazhai, the highest peak of Danxia Mountain, is 619.2 meters high. Danxia Mountain is famous for its red cliffs and extolled as "The Redstone Park in China". It ranks the top among the four famous mountains in Guangdong.

Danxia Mountain Scenic Area has been open to public since 1980. In 1988, it was approved by the State Council as the National Park of China. In 2004 and 2010, it entered the list of UNESCO Global GeoPark and World Natural Heritage respectively. In 2011, it became the National 5A Scenic Area.

Developed tourist area covers Danxia Mountain in the north region and Bazhai Scenic Area in the west, including Zhanglao Peak, Yangyuan Mountain, the Flying Dragon Lake-Lying Dragon Hill scenic area and Jinjiang River Corridor.

Now we are visiting Zhanglao Peak. It can be divided into three layers: upper, middle and bottom layer. Let's go to the bottom layer first to visit Jinshi Rock grotto. It is also a time-honored bodhimanda and an important topographical research route. Then we reach the middle layer to visit Biechuan Temple, Loving Birds Tree and "Red Stairs with Iron Chains". At last, we can hike up to the top layer to enjoy cloud sea, sunrise and sunset glow in the Sun Viewing Pavilion. In the south, there are Yinyuan Stone, the Flying Dragon Lake and Xianju Rock temple.

Now we are seeing Jinshi Rock. Major scenic spots include Dream Awaken Pass, Secluded Cave Leading to Sky, Thin Strip of Sky, Jinyan Rock and so on.

Dream Awaken Pass is a large honeycomb weathering cave. It is 6 meters long, 2 meters high and 2.5 meters deep. A lay Buddhist called Fayun in the Song Dynasty discovered this cave when visiting Jinshi Rock. He thought that the grotesque shape and good environment made the place a perfect area for Buddhism practice. Being reluctant to leave, he exclaimed that "Half a lifetime of running around was like a dream; until today I am awaken and find inner peace." Later people called the cave "Dream Awaken Pass".

In front of us is "Secluded Cave Leading to Sky". It is a natural weathering cave. Passing through the cave, you can see the longest, highest and most splendid "Thin Strip of Sky" in China. The gorge is over 200 meters long and over 70 meters high. The narrowest area here is only 70 centimeters wide. Move ahead you will see the Golden-ripple Jade Lake and the Jade Spring, and then we arrive at Jinyan Rock.

Jinyan Rock is formed by several caves connecting with each other. There are Seven Buddha Hall, the Guanyin Hall and Main Shrine Hall. The cave with the Guanyin Hall is the biggest with 32 Guanyin sculptures of different images inside. The cave is spacious enough to allow hundreds of people worshiping at the same time.

Let's look at the cliffs of the Main Shrine Hall and you will see the "Dragon Scale in Autumn Moon". In spring, the cliffs are light green. In summer they turn into dark green-yellow green in autumn and brown yellow in winter. Because blue-green algae cover the cliffs and they have a strong capacity of absorbing water. The more water they absorb, the darker green color they will show. Otherwise, they turn into light brown yellow. They are also called "chameleon".

Now let's enjoy cliff carving in Danxia Mountain. These two Chinese characters "Jin" and "Yan" are written by Zhao Rulei in the Song Dynasty. This is also the earliest Danxia cliff carving. Cliff carving in Danxia Mountain approved as a Major Historical and Cultural Site

Protected at the National Level in 2013.

We are moving to the middle layer.

The first is Biechuan Temple. Built in 1662, it is famous for Zen's words that "Buddhism learning should not be constraint to words. Heart-to-heart enlightenment is also valued."

This is Loving Birds Tree. It is actually a thitmin and a banyan intertwining with each other. As a poem goes "On high, we'd be two love birds flying wing to wing; on earth, two trees with branches twined from spring to spring." It is said that lovers who join hands and walk around the tree for three times can enjoy a happy marriage forever.

Let's take a break in Yufeng Pavilion and then challenge "Red Stairs with Iron Chains". It is said that a trip to Danxia Mountain without visiting the "Red Stairs with Iron Chains" and Zhanglao Peak is not finished. You can see four Chinese characters "Yi Ruo Deng Tian" and there is one point missing of "Yi". It is not wrongly written. Actually, one point missing in Chinese means "almost reaching the sky", which implies the danger of climbing here.

Now we have reached the Sun Viewing Pavilion in the top layer. As a perfect sightseeing point, it allows visitors to enjoy sunrise in the morning and sunset glow in the evening. Look at the east, that is the famous Monk Hat Peak. In the east there are Wanglanggui Peak, the Pagoda Peak and the Candle Peak. In the south we can see the Golden Turtle Peak, Camel Peak and Shaoshi Mountain. In the west there are Sisters Peak, Jade Kettle Peak, Bazhai Peak, the Skyward Dragon Peak and the Peak of Child-giving Guanyin. In the north you can see the Sleeping Beauty Peak and the Elephants Crowd Mountain. Here you can also enjoy the Snow Rock, Conch Peak, Pearl Peak and so on.

That's the end of my commentary. Wish you a happy journey. Thank you!

四、综合知识

☆丹霞山先后被评为国家级风景名胜区、国家级自然保护区、国家地质公园、国家5A级旅游景区；2004年经联合国教科文组织批准为全球首批世界地质公园；2010年8月，丹霞山联合多地区以"中国丹霞"项目被列为世界自然遗产，成为广东省唯一的世界自然遗产。

☆丹霞山景区丹山、碧水、绿树、田园交相辉映，以"雄、奇、险、秀、幽"著称，是广东四大名山之首。"广东四大名山"即罗浮山、丹霞山、西樵山、鼎湖山。

☆丹霞山由红色砂砾岩构成，整体呈现一种红层峰林式结构，以顶平、身陡、麓缓为特征，赤壁丹崖为典型，其"色如渥丹，灿若明霞"，不同体量和不同形态的赤壁丹崖组成了大小石峰、石堡、石墙、石柱600多座，主峰巴寨海拔619.2米，大多山峰海拔在300～400米之间。

☆丹霞山是丹霞地貌的命名地，也是丹霞地貌发育最典型、类型最齐全、风景最优美的区域，被称为"中国的红石公园"。在一亿年前，丹霞山还是一个大湖泊，随着雨水冲刷而来的沙石、黏土，积聚在了湖盆中。在喜马拉雅山造山运动的影响下，地壳上升，湖底被抬升为山地，富含铁质的沉积物强烈氧化，形成紫红褐色的岩石，在千万年的风化侵蚀作用下，就成了今天的丹霞山。

☆丹霞山全部植物共2270种，可谓"植物王国"。其中丹霞山本地特有种中，丹霞梧桐、丹霞兰、丹霞小花苣苔最为突出和具有代表性。被国家重点保护野生植物名录（1999年）记载的有13种，其中仙湖苏铁为Ⅰ级重点保护植物。

☆早在新石器时代就有古越先民在这里生活，留下了鲶鱼转遗址。丹霞山附近的古越族先民，很早以前就利用天然岩洞结庐而居，山上保留了各个历史时期的古山寨，有"逢山有寨，逢寨有门，逢门必险"的说法。

☆细美寨建于明崇祯年间，主体部分位于阳元山西麓，有三重山门和沿山脊线修凿的石梯，堡寨筑于阳元山顶部，四面为绝壁，山顶筑有水池，易守难攻，现为广东省文物保护单位。

☆丹霞山摩崖石刻于2013年被列为第七批全国重点文物保护单位。在丹霞山通天峡、别传寺、梦觉关、锦石岩等一带，留有自北宋至民国年间的摩崖石刻111题，其中宋刻8处、元刻9处，以"锦岩""丹霞""别有天"等大字摩崖最具代表。宋朝赵汝耒题写的"锦岩"二字是丹霞山现存最早的摩崖石刻。

☆1928年初，朱德、陈毅等率南昌起义军余部经丹霞山第二次到仁化；抗日战争时期，舵石下的朝阳岩及洪岩等成为抗日军民补给地和疗伤地，燕岩成为河富抗战自卫队指挥部驻地。

☆长老峰由长老峰、海螺峰、宝珠峰三峰构成连体山块，由三级绝壁和三级崖坎构成三个最典型的赤壁丹霞景观层次。下层景观以锦石岩为中心，主要景点有梦觉关、幽洞通天、一线天、锦岩、龙鳞片石等。中层景观以别传寺为中心，主要景点有别传寺、杰阁晨钟、竹坡烟雨、一线天、鸳鸯树等。顶层景观以观日亭、宝珠峰东部观景台（韶音亭）为中心，主要景点有丹梯铁索、丹霞观日、韶音亭、舵石等。

☆锦石岩由千圣岩、祖师岩、伏虎岩和龙王岩四岩组成，因岩内石壁万色交错而得名。洞的内壁有一条岩石皱起为蜂窝形的纹路，就像一条鳞甲鲜明的巨龙穿插缠绕于岩洞中。这些惟妙惟肖的"龙鳞"表面附生着蓝藻等生物，可随气温、湿度的变化而改变颜色，春季为嫩绿色，夏季为深绿色，秋季为黄绿色，冬季为黄褐色，被称为"变色龙鳞""龙鳞片石"。

☆梦觉关是一个大型蜂窝状风化洞穴，岩穴长6米、进深2.5米、高2米。据传，佛教居士法云在其洞休憩后，发出"半生奔波如梦幻，今日方觉此清虚！"的感叹，后人遂将该洞取名为"梦觉关"。

☆"幽洞通天"是一个自然风化的岩洞，有我国已发现最长、最高、最壮观的"一线天"，峡长200多米，高70多米，最窄处仅有0.7米。

☆丹霞山是岭南著名宗教圣地。据传，在秦汉时期，就有得道真人道元在混元洞、狮子岩一带修行。隋唐时期开始有僧尼经营，在明清时期达到最盛。目前已发现石窟寺遗存达40多处，有锦石寺、别传寺、雪岩寺等。

☆别传寺被誉为岭南十大丛林之一。清康熙元年（1662年），明遗民澹归来丹霞山开辟道场，建佛堂精舍，以佛教禅宗"教外别传，不立文字"之意，将寺命名为别传寺。澹归自充监院，在别传寺15年，从学弟子最多时达数百人。澹归撰有《绕丹霞记》《丹霞山新建山门记》《丹霞施田碑记》等。

☆鸳鸯树生长在六祖堂旧址旁边。两树远看如一体，枝叶婆娑不分彼此；近看则可辨清树干一里一外，两种不同科属的树相互依存。里面的是百日青，属罗汉松科，外面的是笔管榕，属桑科。它们树叶交错，如同情侣互相拥抱，因此前人以"鸳鸯"命名此树。

☆丹梯通过石阶连接中层和上层，右下方石壁上镌刻"宜若登天"四字。"宜若登天"的"宜"字少了一点，取其"差一点可登天"之意，暗寓其险犹如登天。

韶关市丹霞山景区

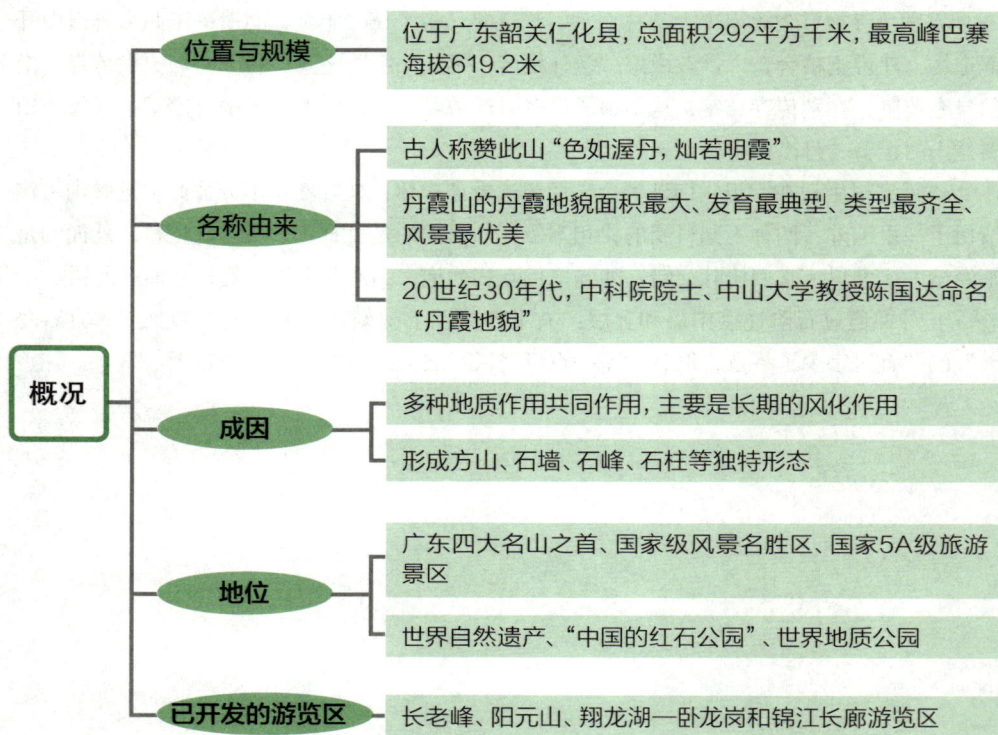

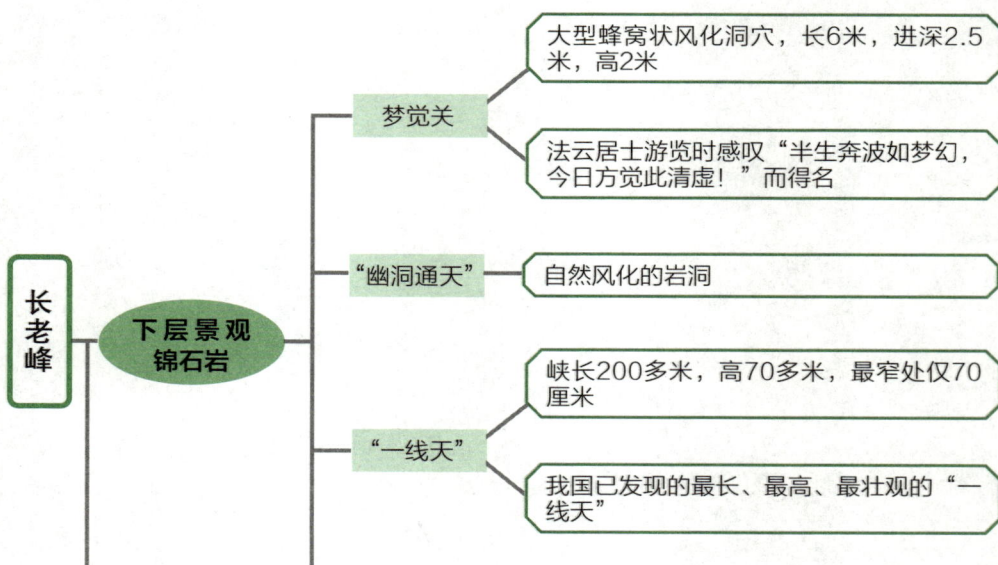

概况

- **位置与规模** —— 位于广东韶关仁化县，总面积292平方千米，最高峰巴寨海拔619.2米

- **名称由来**
  - 古人称赞此山"色如渥丹，灿若明霞"
  - 丹霞山的丹霞地貌面积最大、发育最典型、类型最齐全、风景最优美
  - 20世纪30年代，中科院院士、中山大学教授陈国达命名"丹霞地貌"

- **成因**
  - 多种地质作用共同作用，主要是长期的风化作用
  - 形成方山、石墙、石峰、石柱等独特形态

- **地位**
  - 广东四大名山之首、国家级风景名胜区、国家5A级旅游景区
  - 世界自然遗产、"中国的红石公园"、世界地质公园

- **已开发的游览区** —— 长老峰、阳元山、翔龙湖—卧龙岗和锦江长廊游览区

长老峰

- **下层景观 锦石岩**
  - 梦觉关
    - 大型蜂窝状风化洞穴，长6米，进深2.5米，高2米
    - 法云居士游览时感叹"半生奔波如梦幻，今日方觉此清虚！"而得名
  - "幽洞通天" —— 自然风化的岩洞
  - "一线天"
    - 峡长200多米，高70多米，最窄处仅70厘米
    - 我国已发现的最长、最高、最壮观的"一线天"

数个相连的天然洞穴，分别建有七佛殿、观音殿、大雄宝殿等

丹霞十二景之"片鳞秋月"
- "变色龙"：春嫩绿，夏深绿，秋黄绿，冬褐黄
- 吸水性强，潮湿天吸水越多，越深绿，干旱季节吸水少，呈淡淡的褐黄色

锦岩

观音殿：岩洞最大，可容纳数百善信同时参拜，洞内塑有观音32相

丹霞山现存最早的摩崖石刻"锦岩"二字，宋朝赵汝末题写

中层景观
- 别传寺 —— 建于清康熙元年，因禅宗"不立文字，心印别传"而得名
- 鸳鸯树 —— 百日青和笔管榕两棵树缠绕组成
- 丹梯铁索 —— 宜若登天："宜"字少了一点，取其"差一点可登天"之意，暗寓其险犹如登天

上层景观 观日亭
- 东面：僧帽峰、望郎归、宝塔峰、蜡烛峰
- 南面：金龟回头、骆驼峰、韶石山群峰
- 西面：姐妹峰、玉壶峰、巴寨、朝天龙、送子观音
- 北面：睡美人、群象出山
- 山顶：雪岩、海螺峰、宝珠峰、虹桥拥翠、舵石朝曦

第七节　梅州市叶剑英纪念园

一、讲解要点

（一）概述

1.叶剑英纪念园的地理位置和地位。

2.叶剑英纪念园的构成。

（二）叶剑英纪念馆

1.入口广场：墓志铭、汉白玉方碑。

2.牌坊：对联、浮雕墙。

3.纪念馆：坐姿铜像、到访国家领导人、纪念馆布局结构、陈列展品。

4.叶剑英生平：发动南昌起义、领导广州起义、三次伟大贡献。

二、中文讲解词示例

【欢迎词】

各位游客，大家好！欢迎来到叶剑英纪念园参观。

【概述】

叶剑英纪念园位于梅州市梅县区雁洋镇虎形村，是全国重点文物保护单位、全国爱国主义教育示范基地、全国红色旅游经典景区、国家4A级旅游景区。叶剑英纪念园规划占地面积48200平方米，融客家民居和现代建筑于一体，分为纪念景区、人文秀区、生态林区和旅游休闲服务区四个区域，"少怀壮志""泉井情深""力挽狂澜""翰墨飘香""百战归来"五大主题，是一个展现伟人风范、弘扬客家文化、推进生态旅游的景区。纪念园分为四个部分，展现叶剑英伟大光辉的一生，包括入口广场、牌坊、纪念广场、叶剑英纪念馆等。

【入口广场】

我们现在所在的位置是叶剑英纪念园的入口广场。广场正中的基座上雕刻着"叶剑英纪念园"6个大字。基座前的这块墨绿色长条碑石上，镌刻着中共中央于1987年为叶剑英元帅撰写的墓志铭。立在水池中央的汉白玉方碑四面都雕刻着图案，正面是一级解放勋章，左边是一级八一勋章，右边是一级独立自由勋章，背面则是毛泽东对叶剑英元帅的评价、陈毅元帅亲笔题写的"诸葛一生唯谨慎，吕端大事不糊涂"。

【牌坊】

牌坊正面的对联"剑气凌云精忠社稷叱咤风云铁马啸，英才盖世满腹良谋匡扶政局国基安"巧妙地把叶帅的名字嵌入了对联当中，横额上刻着"盛德若愚"，背面则是"风范长存"，赞扬叶剑英在艰难曲折的革命历程中为中国革命所作出的突出贡献。

浮雕墙"少怀壮志"景观，展现了叶帅青少年时期在家乡的生活。"泉井情深"景观展示的是叶帅74岁回到阔别几十年的家乡，在这里掬起一捧清泉，回忆童年趣事。

【叶剑英纪念馆】

现在我们来到的是纪念馆，这里安放着叶剑英坐姿铜像。叶帅手拿草帽，坐在石头上，面带微笑，亲切慈祥。

叶剑英纪念馆于1989年10月22日落成开馆，由原国家主席杨尚昆题写馆名。开馆以来，纪念馆接待过江泽民、温家宝、乔石、张德江、李岚清、李长春、杨尚昆、王震等党和国家领导人。

纪念馆平面呈矩形与马蹄形组合，占地约1万平方米，建筑风格为客家民居和现代园林相结合，独树一帜。大门外墙两边镶嵌着反映叶剑英元帅生平事迹的汉白玉浮雕，纪念馆序厅里有叶剑英元帅铜像，这座主题雕塑高3.8米，重近2吨，后面背景画的寓意是：在惊涛骇浪的政治风云变幻中，叶剑英元帅为党和国家所作的重大贡献。

纪念馆分为四个展厅，厅内共用照片600多幅、珍贵文献144份、实物近百件，分9个章节，充分向世人展现叶剑英伟大光辉的一生。

纪念馆陈列大楼里的展览内容分为两部分，一是"叶剑英伟大光辉的一生"，一是"叶剑英办公室、卧室实物陈列"。

【叶剑英生平】

叶剑英生于1897年4月28日。1917年，20岁的叶剑英考入云南讲武堂学习，毕业后追随孙中山先生投身民主革命。1924年初，叶剑英受廖仲恺先生邀请，参与创立黄埔陆军军官学校，任教授部副主任。1927年蒋介石发动反革命政变，叶剑英毅然通电反蒋，随即奔赴武汉，任国民革命军第四军参谋长。7月，他在严重的白色恐怖中秘密加入中国共产党。1927年8月1日，叶剑英与周恩来、叶挺、贺龙、刘伯承等发动了南昌起义，12月11日，他与张太雷、叶挺等领导了广州起义。这次广州起义和南昌起义、秋收起义相连接，成为第二次国内革命战争与创立中国工农红军的伟大开端。

在叶帅的一生中，他三次为人民作出了特殊的伟大贡献。第一次，1927年7月下旬，在南昌起义前夕，他冒着生命危险送情报给叶挺等起义领导人，粉碎了国民党企图剿灭起义部队的阴谋。第二次，1935年9月9日，在长征途中，当他获悉张国焘阴谋策划用武力控制以毛泽东为首的党中央后，立即报告了毛泽东，使党中央及时安全转移，挽救了党中央。第三次，1976年秋，叶帅与中央其他领导人一起，一举粉碎了"四人帮"反党集团，党和国家转危为安。

叶剑英元帅于1986年10月22日因病在北京逝世，享年89岁。在半个多世纪的革命斗争中，叶剑英为中国人民的解放事业和社会主义事业兢兢业业，英勇奋斗，建立了无数丰功伟绩。他是中华人民共和国德高望重的开国元勋之一，是我们党、国家和军队的一位杰出领导人，他的一生是伟大光辉的一生。

【结束语】

叶剑英纪念园的讲解到此结束，谢谢大家！

三、英文讲解词示例

Ye Jianying Memorial Park, Meizhou

Hello, everyone!

Welcome to the Ye Jianying Memorial Park. This Memorial Park is one of China's Major Historical and Cultural Sites Protected at the National Level, and it is a National 4A Scenic Area, located in Huxing Village, Yanyang Town, Mei County, Meizhou. Besides, it has been listed as the National Demonstration Base for Patriotic Education, and one of the National Red Tourism Scenic Area. With the integration of traditional Hakka houses and modern buildings, this 48,200-square-meter Memorial Park contains four areas, which are the memorial area, cultural area, green landscape area, and tourism and service area. The hall presents Marshal Ye's life under five key themes: "Noble Aspirations in Youth", "Spring Well", "Guardian of Leadership", "Fragrance of Calligraphy", and "Returning Hometown".

We are now standing in the Entrance Square. In the center of the square, there is a pedestal inscribed with the six characters "Ye Jian Ying Ji Nian Yuan", which means Ye Jianying Memorial Park. The long, dark green stone tablet before us is engraved with the epitaph written by the Central Committee of the Communist Party of China in 1987 for Marshal Ye. Let's look at the white marble stele in the center of the pool. All four sides are carved with patterns—there are medals awarded to Marshal Ye on its front, left, and right side; the back displays Chairman Mao's comment of Ye, "Zhuge Liang was cautious his whole life through, while Lv Duan stayed clear when big matters were due", written by Marshal Chen Yi himself.

You can see on the front of the Memorial Gate, there is a couplet, saying "Jian Qi Ling Yun Jing Zhong She Ji Chi Zha Feng Yun Tie Ma Xiao, Ying Cai Gai Shi Man Fu Liang Mou Kuang Fu Zheng Ju Guo Ji An." Means "With sword in hand, for country and land, he stood so grand; a genius born with wisdom, he secured the realm for peace to keep." If you read the first character of each line, "Jian" and "Ying", you can find that is Marshal Ye's name. The horizontal plaque reads "Sheng De Ruo Yu", which means "greatest virtue appears foolish" and on its back is inscribed "Feng Fan Chang Cun" which means "noble legacy endures". All these are praising Marshal Ye's significant contributions to the Chinese revolution during the difficult and challenging course.

The embossed wall with the theme of "Noble Aspirations in Youth" portrays Marshal Ye's life as a young man in his hometown. The landscape with the theme of "Spring Well" commemorates Marshal Ye's return to his hometown at the age of 74 after decades away, where he scooped up a handful of spring water, recalling the joys of his childhood.

Now, we are at Ye Jianying Memorial Hall, where a bronze statue of Ye Jianying in a seated position is displayed. As you can see, he is holding a straw hat and sitting on a stone with a warm and kind smile.

The Hall was completed and opened on October 22, 1989, with the hall's name inscribed by former Chinese President Yang Shangkun.

The floor plan of the Memorial Hall combines rectangular and horseshoe shapes, covering about 10,000 square meters, whose design uniquely integrates traditional Hakka houses with modern garden design. On both sides of the outer wall of the main entrance are white marble reliefs depicting significant events in Marshal Ye's life. Inside the Hall stands a bronze statue of Marshal Ye, a 3.8-meter-tall, nearly 2-ton sculpture. Behind the statue, there is a painting symbolizing the turbulent political waves in which Marshal Ye has made significant contributions to Communist Party of China and the country.

There are four exhibition halls in this Memorial Hall, displaying over 600 photographs, 144 valuable documents, and nearly 100 exhibits, organized into 9 chapters, that fully show Marshal Ye's great and glorious life.

The exhibits in the Hall are generally divided into two parts: one is about *Ye's Great and Glorious Life*; another is about *The Authentic Display of Ye's Office and Bedroom*.

Ye Jianying was born on April 28, 1897. In 1917, at the age of 20, he enrolled in the Yunnan Military Academy. After graduating, he followed Sun Yat-sen and dedicated himself to the democratic revolution. In early 1924, at Liao Zhongkai's invitation, Ye participated in the founding of the Whampoa Military Academy, serving as the deputy director of the education department. In 1927, when Chiang Kai-shek launched a counter-revolutionary coup, Ye resolutely opposed him and soon moved to Wuhan, where he served as the Chief of Staff of the Fourth Army of the National Revolutionary Army. In July, amid the intense "White Terror", he secretly joined the Communist Party of China. On August 1, 1927, Ye, along with Zhou Enlai, Ye Ting, He Long, and Liu Bocheng, led the Nanchang Uprising. On December 11, he, along with Zhang Tailei, Ye Ting, and others, led the Guangzhou Uprising. This uprising, along with the Nanchang Uprising and the Autumn Harvest Uprising, marked the beginning of Agrarian Revolutionary War and the founding of the Chinese Workers' and Peasants' Red Army.

Throughout Marshal Ye's life, he made three outstanding contributions to the people. The first was in late July 1927, on the eve of the Nanchang Uprising, when he risked his life delivering messages to Ye Ting and other uprising leaders, smashing the Kuomintang's plot to crush the rebel forces. The second was on September 9, 1935, during the Long March, when he reported Zhang Guotao's plan to use force against the Central Committee led by Mao Zedong, enabling the safe relocation of the Central Committee and saving the leadership. The third was in the autumn of 1976, when Ye, together with other leaders in the Central Committee, played a crucial role in overthrowing the "Gang of Four", thereby stabilizing the Party and the nation.

Marshal Ye Jianying passed away in Beijing on October 22, 1986, at the age of 89. He was one of the esteemed founding fathers of the People's Republic of China and a distinguished leader of the Party, state, and army. His life was a great and glorious one.

This concludes our tour of the Ye Jianying Memorial Park. Thank you for your attention!

四、综合知识

☆叶剑英纪念园位于梅州市梅县区雁洋镇虎形村，虎形村其形似虎，头饮梅江水，背靠虎形山，风光旖旎，山明水秀，是中国人民解放军的缔造者之一、中华人民共和国开国元勋叶剑英的故乡。梅州是具有光荣传统的革命老区，也是广东唯一的全区域被认定为原中央苏区的地级市。

☆叶剑英纪念园融客家民居与现代园林建筑风格于一体，是在原叶剑英元帅故居和纪念馆的基础上进行整合、扩建和充实起来的，分为纪念景区、人文秀区、生态林区和旅游休闲服务区四个部分。是全国重点文物保护单位、全国爱国主义教育示范基地、全国红色旅游经典景区，2008年被评为国家4A级旅游景区。

☆人文秀区以叶剑英故居、叶家宗祠为核心，展示叶剑英出生和成长的环境。生态林区中结合山道布置"叶道英亭""心系赤子"石刻等。旅游休闲服务区内设置模拟军事训练基地、植物园、客家风情街、农家乐园。

☆叶剑英故居原有15间房子，其中4间为叶剑英家所有，左侧2间是叶剑英少年时的卧室和书房。

☆纪念景区在纪念园西部，分为"少怀壮志""泉井情深""力挽狂澜""翰墨飘香""百战归来"五大主题，包括入口广场、牌坊、纪念广场、叶剑英纪念馆等部分。入口广场正中的基座上雕刻着"叶剑英纪念园"6个大字。基座前的这块墨绿色长条碑石上，镌刻着中共中央于1987年为叶剑英元帅撰写的墓志铭。

☆纪念园正大门两边为金黄色墙体，入口广场正中建一水池，中央建一座石雕，镶嵌一块石碑。进入大门，迎面是一座牌坊，牌坊正面的对联"剑气凌云精忠社稷叱咤风云铁马啸，英才盖世满腹良谋匡扶政局国基安"，横额"盛德若愚"，背面则是"风范长存"。

☆立在水池中央的汉白玉方碑四面都雕刻着图案，正面是一级解放勋章，左边是一级八一勋章，右边是一级独立自由勋章，背面则是毛泽东对叶剑英元帅的评价、陈毅元帅亲笔题写的"诸葛一生唯谨慎，吕端大事不糊涂"。

☆叶剑英曾多次在重大历史关头挺身而出，力挽狂澜。1922年，叶剑英护卫孙中山脱险；1927年，叶剑英与周恩来、叶挺、贺龙、刘伯承等发动南昌起义；1935年，叶剑英机智勇敢地同张国焘分裂红军、危害党中央的阴谋作斗争，为党中央和红军胜利北上立了大功；1976年，叶剑英同华国锋、李先念等一道，代表党和人民的意志，粉碎"四人帮"。其中，广州起义、南昌起义、秋收起义是第二次国内革命战争与创立中国工农红军的伟大开端。

☆1935年6月中旬，中央红军与红四方面军会师，决定全体北上抗日。但张国焘不执行北上方针，并发出一封危害和分裂党和红军的密电，这份密电被时任右路军参谋长的叶剑英所截获，他识破了张国焘的阴谋，立即报告了毛泽东。在紧急关头，毛泽东带着中央红军先行北上。毛泽东后来多次称赞叶剑英在这一关键时刻"救了党，救了红军"。

☆叶剑英纪念馆于1989年10月22日落成开馆，由原国家主席杨尚昆题写馆名。2001年，叶剑英纪念馆由中共中央宣传部公布为全国爱国主义教育示范基地。

☆纪念馆序厅屹立的叶剑英元帅铜像拄杖站立，挺拔威严，令人肃然起敬。馆内共分为四个展厅，厅内共用照片600多幅，珍贵文献144份，实物近百件；分9个章节，以编年体和小专题相结合的形式陈列。

☆在叶剑英纪念馆内，有一幅《舌战群儒图》油画。画上的叶剑英身穿黄呢子军服，佩戴中将军衔，臂带石膏夹板，但仍精神抖擞，目光如炬，淡定自若。1940年3月，蒋介石在重庆召开全国参谋长会议，时任八路军参谋长的叶剑英参加了会议，集中讲了关于作战和磨擦两个问题，用大量事实介绍八路军、新四军的战绩，驳斥国民党顽固派对八路军、新四军的种种诬蔑。

梅州市叶剑英纪念园

概况

- **位置与规模** —— 梅州市梅县区雁洋镇虎形村, 规划占地面积48200平方米

- **景区组成**
  - 四个部分: 纪念景区、人文秀区、生态林区和旅游休闲服务区
  - 五大主题: "少怀壮志""泉井情深""力挽狂澜""翰墨飘香""百战归来"
  - 功能齐全、综合配套完善的大型旅游休闲度假区和国际会议中心

- **地位** —— 全国重点文物保护单位、全国爱国主义教育示范基地、全国红色旅游经典景区、国家4A级旅游景区

入口广场

- **正中的基座** —— 雕刻"叶剑英纪念园"6个大字

- **基座前墨绿色长条碑石** —— 镌刻叶剑英元帅的墓志铭, 中共中央于1987年撰写

- **立在水池中央的汉白玉方碑**
  - 正面: 一级解放勋章
  - 左边: 一级八一勋章
  - 右边: 一级独立自由勋章
  - 背面: "诸葛一生唯谨慎, 吕端大事不糊涂", 毛泽东的评价, 陈毅亲笔题写

- **牌坊**
  - 正面对联: "剑气凌云精忠社稷叱咤风云铁马啸, 英才盖世满腹良谋匡扶政局国基安"
  - 横额: "盛德若愚"
  - 背面: "风范长存"

- **浮雕墙**
  - "少怀壮志": 叶帅青少年时期在家乡的生活
  - "泉井情深": 叶帅74岁回乡, 曾在这里掬起一捧清泉, 回忆童年趣事

叶剑英纪念馆

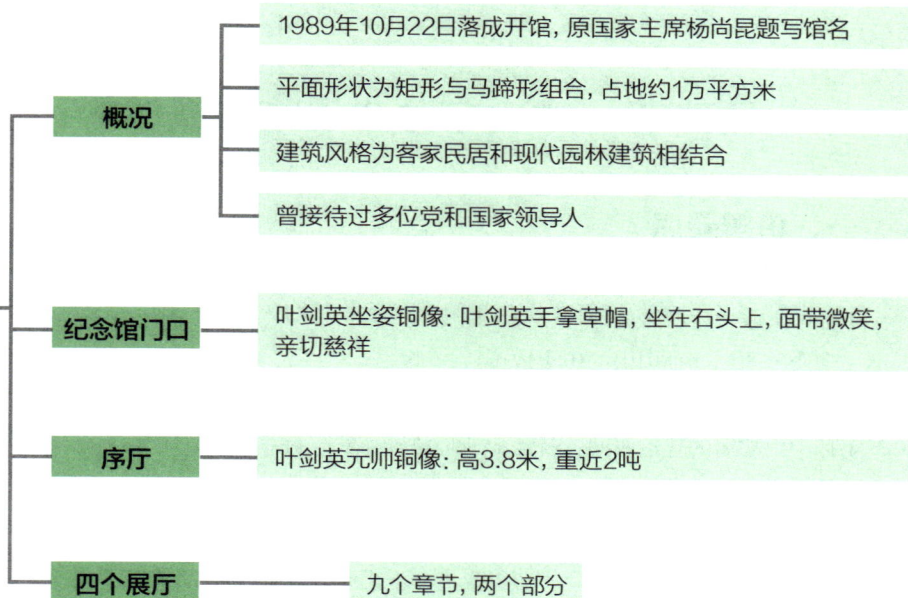

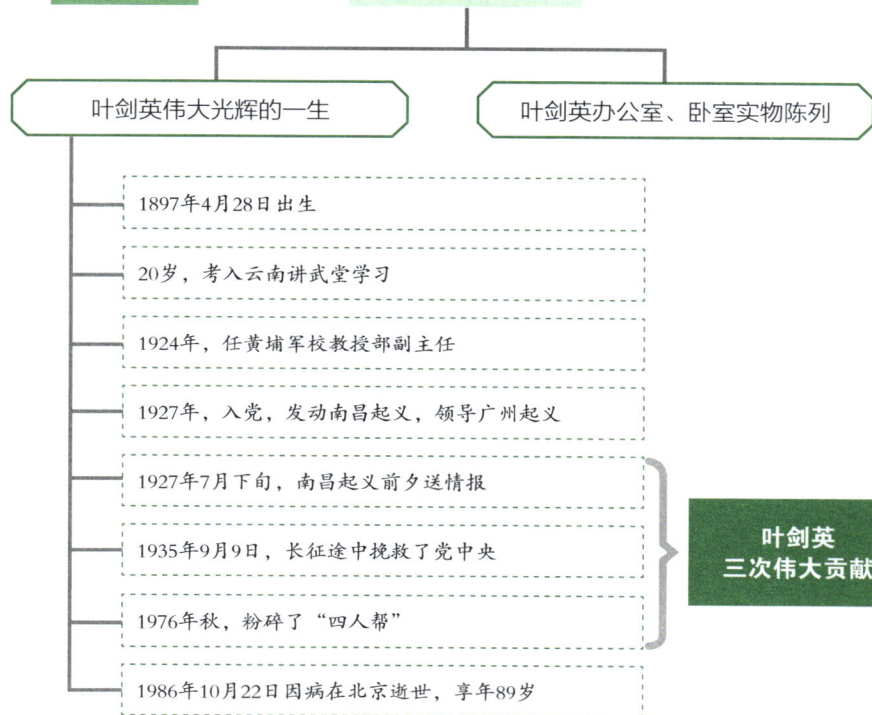

概况
- 1989年10月22日落成开馆, 原国家主席杨尚昆题写馆名
- 平面形状为矩形与马蹄形组合, 占地约1万平方米
- 建筑风格为客家民居和现代园林建筑相结合
- 曾接待过多位党和国家领导人

纪念馆门口
- 叶剑英坐姿铜像: 叶剑英手拿草帽, 坐在石头上, 面带微笑, 亲切慈祥

序厅
- 叶剑英元帅铜像: 高3.8米, 重近2吨

四个展厅
- 九个章节, 两个部分

叶剑英伟大光辉的一生

叶剑英办公室、卧室实物陈列

- 1897年4月28日出生
- 20岁, 考入云南讲武堂学习
- 1924年, 任黄埔军校教授部副主任
- 1927年, 入党, 发动南昌起义, 领导广州起义
- 1927年7月下旬, 南昌起义前夕送情报
- 1935年9月9日, 长征途中挽救了党中央
- 1976年秋, 粉碎了"四人帮"
- 1986年10月22日因病在北京逝世, 享年89岁

叶剑英
三次伟大贡献

第八节　中山市孙中山故里旅游区

一、讲解要点

（一）概述

1.孙中山故里旅游区的地理位置、地位、展区。

2.宋庆龄题词和孙中山的历史地位。

（二）孙中山故居

1.孙中山故居的建造时间、特点、地理位置，翠亨村。

2.孙中山的出生处。

3.孙中山故居屋前的酸子树、大门对联、客厅、卧室、厨房、浴室、厕所。

（三）孙中山纪念馆

1.孙中山纪念馆的建筑荣誉。

2.展览的分布和简介。

二、中文讲解词示例

【欢迎词】

各位来宾大家好！欢迎来到孙中山故里旅游区参观游览。

【概述】

孙中山故里旅游区位于广东省中山市南朗镇翠亨村，包括孙中山故居纪念馆、翠亨村、中山城、辛亥革命纪念公园和犁头尖山五个核心景区，为5A级旅游景区。孙中山故居纪念馆是国家一级博物馆，以"孙中山及其成长的社会环境"为主题，有孙中山纪念展示区，包括孙中山故居和孙中山纪念馆；还有辛亥革命纪念公园，农耕文化展示区，非物质文化遗产展示区，翠亨民居展示区，杨殷、陆皓东纪念展示区，孙中山廉政思想及实践展览等展区。还是中山市孙中山研究所和中山市民俗博物馆。

现在我们看到的这个"中山故居公园"木匾，是1959年8月孙中山夫人、国家名誉主席宋庆龄的题词。

孙中山先生是伟大的民主革命先驱，他领导的辛亥革命推翻了在中国延续了两千多年的封建帝制，建立了中国和亚洲历史上第一个共和国，他的三民主义（民族、民权、民生）思想理论体系，要求实现民族独立，建立共和，成为20世纪初期全面推动中国社会进步的伟大思想纲领。

【孙中山故居】

我们眼前这座建筑就是孙中山故居，是1892年由孙中山的大哥孙眉出资、孙中山主持建造的，是全国重点文物保护单位。它有三个特点：一是中西合璧，外洋内中；二是坐东朝西；三是门多窗多，回环连通。

孙中山故居位于翠亨村的边缘。翠亨村走出了孙中山、杨鹤龄、杨殷、陆皓东等历史名人，是中国历史文化名村、中国传统村落。村里现在大约还有100户人家。

不过，这个两层的楼房并非孙中山的诞生地。大家看一下故居前面的这口水井，水井旁原有一间房子，1866年11月12日孙中山就出生在这所小房子里。1892年建成新居后，孙家便拆掉了原来的房子。孙中山在这里出生，并在这里度过了他的童年和青少年的大部分时间。1925年3月12日，孙中山先生在北京逝世。

故居前的这棵树叫酸子树，是孙中山先生1883年从檀香山带回来种子并种植在这里的，至今已有140多岁，见证了故居的历史沧桑。

故居大门的对联"一椽得所，五桂安居"是孙中山手迹。椽是屋顶盖瓦片的木板，孙中山谦虚地用"一椽得所"来形容这是一块木板那么大的房子。"五桂安居"是在五桂山脚下安居乐业的意思——因为翠亨村就位于五桂山脚下。

现在大家随我进入故居参观。1892年新居建成后至1895年，孙中山在珠三角一带行医和从事革命活动，经常居住在这里。1912年5月，孙中山辞去临时大总统职务后回乡考察，也是住在这里。

一楼的客厅正面是孙中山的画像，是他在1912年担任临时大总统时的形象，两边墙上是他父母的画像。上面的神龛，是供奉菩萨和祖先牌位的地方。

右边耳房是孙中山的卧室，现在大家看到的大木床、梳妆台和凳等，还原了当年的生活起居场景。经过孙中山先生的卧室，我们来到厨房。

孙家的厨房建于1913年，现在陈设的是孙家的碗柜和加工粮食的工具等。厨房外面还设有浴室，浴室的浴缸是孙中山先生从海外购买回来的。浴室对面有一间厕所。当年孙家因地制宜，家里使用的是旱厕，也就是柴灰马桶。马桶下面堆放厨房柴炉的柴灰，定期清理作为有机肥使用，既环保又没有异味。

【孙中山纪念馆】

孙中山纪念馆是陈列展览综合楼，该建筑内外风格浑然一体，与展览协调统一，一落成就荣获中国建筑装饰行业最高荣誉奖——全国建筑工程装饰奖和全国十大陈列展览精品奖。

展馆的序厅，展现的是一位"平民总统"的形象，孙中山铜像站立在孙中山故居院门前，一个农家子弟赤脚从这里走向世界，中国的民主共和制度从这里开始。

展馆首层布置了"孙中山生平史绩"陈列，介绍了孙中山为创立共和、捍卫共和而奋斗一生的伟大事迹，全面、系统地介绍了孙中山的革命精神、伟大人格、思想理论和他领导的革命运动，永远纪念他领导人民推翻帝制、建立共和国的丰功伟绩。展馆还介绍了孙中山革命事业主要追随者的情况。

二楼展厅布置了"孙中山亲属与后裔"陈列，反映了孙中山亲属对革命事业的支持、贡献和牺牲，介绍了孙中山后裔的相关情况。

二楼设有逸仙图书馆和孙中山研究信息中心，还设置有临时展厅，不定期举办一些展览。

【结束语】

我的讲解到此结束，谢谢大家！

三、英文讲解词示例

Sun Yat-sen Hometown Scenic Spot, Zhongshan

Hello, everyone! Welcome to Sun Yat-sen Hometown Scenic Spot! We're delighted to have you here.

Sun Yat-sen Hometown Scenic Spot is located in Cuiheng Village, Nanlang Town, Zhongshan, Guangdong Province. It is one of National 5A Scenic Areas. The spot consists of five core zones, namely Sun Yat-sen's Former Residence Memorial Museum, Cuiheng Village, Zhongshan Town, the 1911 Revolution Memorial Park, and the Litoujian Mountain.

Sun Yat-sen's Former Residence Memorial Museum is a National First-Level Museum, the theme of which focuses on Sun Yat-sen's life and the social environment for his upbringing. The Sun Yat-sen Memorial Exhibition Area of the museum includes Sun Yat-sen's former residence and Dr. Sun Yat-sen Memorial Museum. The museum also features other exhibition areas, such as the 1911 Revolution Memorial Park, the Farming Culture Exhibition Area, Intangible Cultural Heritage Exhibition Area, Cuiheng Civil Residence Exhibition Area, Cuiheng Village Area, and the Yang Yin and Lu Haodong Memorial Exhibition Area. Also, the museum is known as Zhongshan Institute for Sun Yat-sen Studies and Zhongshan Folklore Museum.

The wooden plaque you see here inscribed with "Sun Yat-sen Former Residence Park", "Zhong Shan Gu Ju Gong Yuan" in Chinese was penned in August 1959 by Madam Soong Ching-ling, Sun Yat-sen's wife and the Honorary President of China.

Sun Yat-sen was a great pioneer of the Chinese democratic revolution. The 1911 Revolution in 1911 led by him overthrew the feudal monarchy which lasted over 2,000 years and established the first republic in China and Asia. "Three Principles of the People—Nationalism, Democracy, and People's Livelihood" is the main theory proposed by Sun. The call for national independence and the determination to build a republic of China based on the theory has made a complete ideology system of his, which has played a vital role in driving the progress of Chinese society in the early 20th century.

The building in front of us is Sun Yat-sen's former residence, built in 1892 with funds from his elder brother, Sun Mei, and overseen by himself. It is a Major Historical and Cultural Site Protected at the National Level. The building has three features. First, it is a combination of Chinese and Western styles. The building outlook is western style but the decoration inside is Chinese style. Second, it faces west with its back to the west. The third one is many windows and doors are installed, connecting all the rooms.

The residence is located on the outskirts of Cuiheng Village, a village of significant historical and cultural importance in China. Currently, about 100 households reside in the village.

However, this two-floors building is not where Sun Yat-sen was born. Can you see the well in front of us? There used to be a small house beside it. That's where Sun was born on November 12, 1866. The original house was demolished after the new residence was completed in 1892. Sun Yat-sen spent his childhood and much of his youth here. He passed away in Beijing on March 12, 1925.

This tree in front of the residence is a tamarind, planted here by Sun Yat-sen with its seed brought back from Honolulu in 1883. Now the tree is over-140 years old having witnessed the history of the residence.

The couplet on its gate, saying "Yi Chuan Suo De, Wu Gui An Ju", which means "A house humble as a rafter; a joy of peace in Wugui." They were written by Sun Yat-sen and in his own handwriting. "Yi Chuan Suo De" literally refers to a single roof beam, which are used here in a modest way by Sun Yat-sen, describing the house as one that is only a single roof beam large. "Wu Gui An Ju" refers to the peaceful life at the foot of Wugui Mountain, where Cuiheng Village is located.

Now, let's enter the house. The house was completed in 1892. Between 1892 and 1895, while practicing medicine and engaging in revolutionary activities in the Pearl River Delta, he spent times here quite a lot. He also returned to stay here in May 1912 after resigning from his position as the provisional President.

The front hall features a portrait of Sun Yat-sen as he appeared in 1912 when he served as the provisional President. On either side walls are portraits of his parents. The altar above is for worshipping the Buddha and the ancestors.

The side room at the right side is Sun's bedroom. As we walk can see the furniture, the large wooden bed, dressing table and stool, you can easily picturize the Sun's daily life here. Next, we will be in the kitchen.

The kitchen was built in 1913. Inside, you'll see the Sun family's cupboard and tools for processing food. There is also a bathroom outside the kitchen, and the bathtub was bought by

Sun from overseas. There is a toilet room opposite the bathroom. At that time, the Sun family adapted to local conditions, built a pit latrine, that is, a wood-ash toilet. The wood ash of the kitchen stove is piled under the toilet, and it is regularly cleaned as an organic fertilizer, which is environmentally friendly and not stinky.

The Sun Yat-sen Memorial Museum, a comprehensive exhibition building, integrates its interior and exterior designs with the displays. Upon completion, it won the highest honor in China's architectural decoration industry—the National Architectural Engineering Decoration Award and earned the title of one of the National Top Ten Exhibitions in China.

The entrance hall presents the image of a "People's President". There is a bronze statue of Sun Yat-sen in front of the gate. Sun, a barefoot country boy walked from this very spot to the world, and initiated China's Democratic Republic.

The first floor of the hall houses the exhibition *Sun Yat-sen's Life and Achievements*, which details his lifelong dedication to establishing and defending the Republic. It provides a comprehensive and systematic overview of his revolutionary spirit, noble character, ideological contributions, and the revolutionary movements he led. This exhibit is a lasting tribute to his monumental role in leading the people to overthrow the imperial system and founding the Republic of China. It also reflects the facts about his major followers in the revolutionary cause.

On the second floor, the exhibition, *Sun Yat-sen's Family and Descendants*, introduces the support, contributions, and sacrifices of Sun's family for the revolutionary cause, and provides information about his descendants.

The second floor houses the Sun Yat-sen Library and the Dr. Sun Yat-sen Research Information Center. And on this floor there is a temporary exhibition hall for various non-scheduled exhibitions. That is all for my introduction. Thank you for your time!

四、综合知识

☆孙中山故里旅游区坐落在广东省中山市翠亨新区（南朗镇）翠亨村，总面积达3.15平方千米，包括孙中山故居纪念馆、翠亨村、中山城、辛亥革命纪念公园和犁头尖山五个核心景区，全方位呈现了孙中山从出生成长到进行革命活动的相关历史遗迹。

☆2016年，孙中山故里旅游区被评为国家5A级旅游景区，是中山市首个国家5A级旅游景区，也是广东省内首个以文化为品牌的国家5A级旅游景区。

☆孙中山故居纪念馆于1956年11月落成，是国家一级博物馆、全国爱国主义教育示范基地，建立了以"孙中山及其成长的社会环境"为主题的展示体系，主要有孙中山纪念展示区、翠亨民居展示区、农耕文化展示区和杨殷、陆皓东纪念展示区。

☆1892年初，孙中山亲自设计和主持修建了一座两层的小楼，就是现在人们所看到的孙中山故居。1986年，孙中山故居公布为全国重点文物保护单位。

☆孙中山故居坐东向西，占地面积约500平方米，建筑面积约340平方米。为砖木结构、中西结合的两层楼房，分前院、主体建筑和后院，并设有一道围墙环绕着庭院。前院右边的水井周围即是孙中山先生诞生时的旧房所在地。故居前院栽植一株酸子树，1883年，孙中山从檀香山带回树种栽种在这里。

☆故居二楼南边，是孙中山的书房，墙上挂着孙中山17岁时的照片，室内有孙中山日常使用过的书桌、台椅、铁床。1893年冬，孙中山曾在此书房草拟《上李鸿章书》，提出"人能尽其才、地能尽其利、物能尽其用、货能畅其流"的主张。1895年，孙中山曾在此书房内与陆皓东商讨救国方略。

☆翠亨民居展示区利用翠亨村一部分旧民居展示孙中山童年时的生活环境，包括复原的孙中山祖居、翠亨村民俗展览以及翠亨村当年各层次的民居、民俗展示。

☆农耕文化展示区在孙中山曾经劳作过的耕地上开辟，包括水稻种植区、作物种植区、禽畜饲养区、传统生态农业的桑基鱼塘区、现代农业试验区、农具展览等，展示孙中山家乡的农耕文化。

☆非物质文化遗产展示区利用翠亨村一部分旧民居展示本地列入国家和广东省非遗保护目录的非物质文化遗产项目。

☆杨殷、陆皓东纪念展示区包括中国共产党早期重要领导人、著名的工人运动领袖杨殷烈士的故居及生平展览，以及被孙中山先生誉为"中国有史以来为共和革命而牺牲者之第一人"的陆皓东烈士的故居及生平纪念展览等。

☆孙中山纪念馆主要陈列孙中山生平史迹及其家族情况。展馆一楼"孙中山生平史迹"陈列全面、系统地介绍孙中山领导的革命运动和思想理论，还介绍了孙中山革命事业主要追随者的情况。展馆二楼"孙中山亲属与后裔"陈列展示了孙中山的亲属与后裔对其革命事业的巨大支持、贡献和牺牲。二楼还设有逸仙图书馆和孙中山研究信息中心，附设专题展厅，定期举办各类专题展览。

☆翠亨村原名蔡坑村，后因附近山林青翠，故改名翠亨村。西为群山起伏的五桂山脉，东临珠江。村里现在大约有100户人家。翠亨村是民主革命先行者孙中山的故乡，孙中山1866年诞生于此，还走出了杨鹤龄（革命志士、民国时期孙中山总统府顾问）、杨殷（中国共产党早期领导人）、陆皓东（民主革命者）等历史名人，是中国历史文化名村、中国传统村落。

☆1883年，孙中山从檀香山回到翠亨村。据说孙中山当时经常集合村中的青少年，演说太平天国和华盛顿、拿破仑的事迹。陆皓东、杨心如等都是他在村中志同道合的同龄朋友，后人把孙中山、陆皓东、杨心如、杨鹤龄合称为"翠亨四杰"。

☆辛亥革命纪念公园集孙中山与辛亥革命纪念、休闲游玩等特色元素于一体。公园整体建筑风格偏向中西合璧，营造色彩丰富、层次立体、花木扶疏的园林空间。花岗岩日记墙刻有孙中山、黄兴、蔡元培、毛泽东、朱德、董必武、宋庆龄等人对辛亥革命历史的日记、回忆录以及诗词等。

中山市孙中山故里旅游区

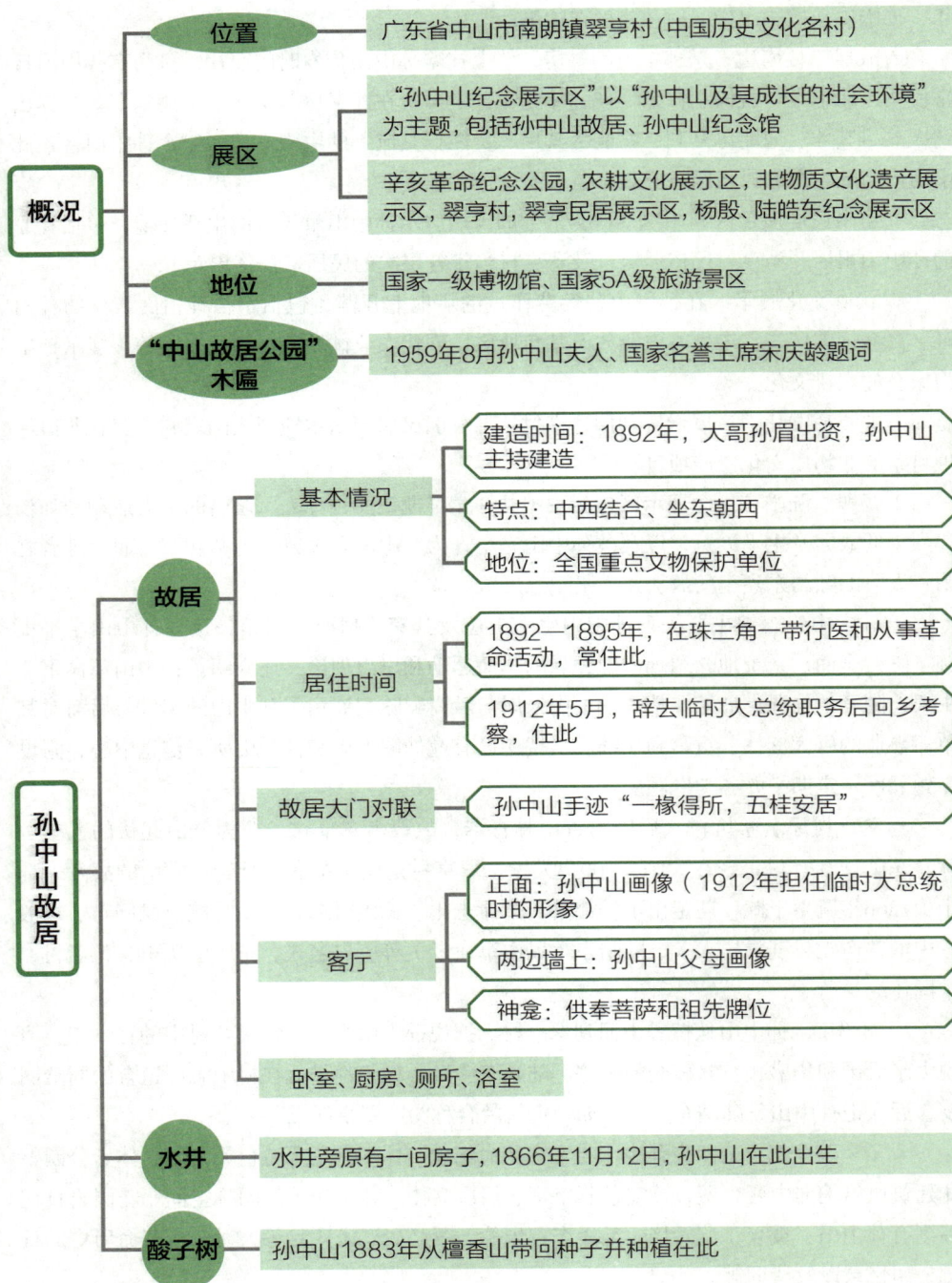

概况

- **位置** —— 广东省中山市南朗镇翠亨村（中国历史文化名村）

- **展区**
  - "孙中山纪念展示区"以"孙中山及其成长的社会环境"为主题，包括孙中山故居、孙中山纪念馆
  - 辛亥革命纪念公园，农耕文化展示区，非物质文化遗产展示区，翠亨村，翠亨民居展示区，杨殷、陆皓东纪念展示区

- **地位** —— 国家一级博物馆、国家5A级旅游景区

- **"中山故居公园"木匾** —— 1959年8月孙中山夫人、国家名誉主席宋庆龄题词

孙中山故居

- **故居**
  - **基本情况**
    - 建造时间：1892年，大哥孙眉出资，孙中山主持建造
    - 特点：中西结合、坐东朝西
    - 地位：全国重点文物保护单位
  - **居住时间**
    - 1892—1895年，在珠三角一带行医和从事革命活动，常住此
    - 1912年5月，辞去临时大总统职务后回乡考察，住此
  - **故居大门对联** —— 孙中山手迹"一椽得所，五桂安居"
  - **客厅**
    - 正面：孙中山画像（1912年担任临时大总统时的形象）
    - 两边墙上：孙中山父母画像
    - 神龛：供奉菩萨和祖先牌位
  - 卧室、厨房、厕所、浴室

- **水井** —— 水井旁原有一间房子，1866年11月12日，孙中山在此出生

- **酸子树** —— 孙中山1883年从檀香山带回种子并种植在此

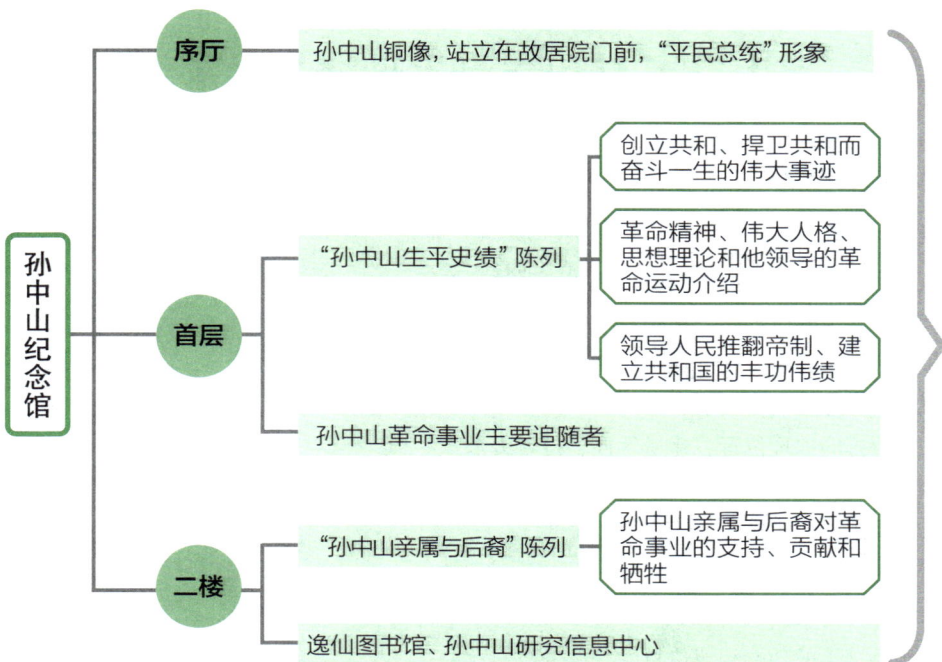

孙中山纪念馆

序厅 —— 孙中山铜像，站立在故居院门前，"平民总统"形象

首层
　　"孙中山生平史绩"陈列
　　　　创立共和、捍卫共和而奋斗一生的伟大事迹
　　　　革命精神、伟大人格、思想理论和他领导的革命运动介绍
　　　　领导人民推翻帝制、建立共和国的丰功伟绩
　　孙中山革命事业主要追随者

二楼
　　"孙中山亲属与后裔"陈列 —— 孙中山亲属与后裔对革命事业的支持、贡献和牺牲
　　逸仙图书馆、孙中山研究信息中心

全国建筑工程装饰奖 全国十大陈列展览精品奖

第九节　江门市开平碉楼与村落

一、讲解要点

（一）概况

1.开平碉楼的地理位置、修建时间、现状、美誉。

2.开平碉楼的修建原因及主要功能。

3.开平碉楼的类型和建筑特点。

（二）自力村碉楼群

1.自力村的地理位置、建造年代、村名由来。

2.自力村碉楼的建筑特点。

3.铭石楼的代表性。

（三）方氏灯楼

1.方氏灯楼的地理位置、建造年代和名称由来。

2.方氏灯楼的功能和建造目的。

二、中文讲解词示例

【欢迎词】

各位游客，大家好！欢迎来到美丽的华侨之乡、碉楼之乡——开平！今天将由我和大家一起去了解开平碉楼建筑。

【概况】

开平碉楼位于广东省江门市下辖的开平市境内，始建于清初，而大量兴建则主要集中在20世纪二三十年代，在鼎盛时期达3300多座。目前，经开平市人民政府普查、登记在册的有1833座。开平碉楼集防卫和居住于一体，融合中西建筑艺术，被誉为"华侨文化的典范之作"。2007年6月28日，开平碉楼被联合国教科文组织列入世界遗产名录，这也是广东省首个世界文化遗产。

为什么要建碉楼呢？一方面是因为地理因素，开平境内多平原，地势低洼，经常会受到台风、洪涝灾害的侵害；另一方面是社会因素，清末民初社会动荡，开平地区长年匪盗横行，为了保护生命和财产安全，当地人便修筑了集防御和居住一体的碉楼。*速记 碉楼建立的原因：地理因素→防洪涝；社会因素→防盗匪。

这些碉楼的造型各异，融合了古希腊、古罗马、伊斯兰等多种风格，中西合璧，百花齐放。按建筑材料可分为石楼、夯土楼、砖楼和混凝土楼四种；按功能分，则有用作家族居住的居楼、村民共同集资兴建的众楼以及主要用于打更放哨的更楼。

开平碉楼尽管在用材、风格上各有差异，但都有一个共同的特点，就是"楼高、墙厚、门窗小"。开平碉楼一般为多层建筑，远远高于平常民居，便于居高临下进行防御。碉楼的墙体比普通的民居厚实坚固，不怕匪盗凿墙或者火攻。有的碉楼顶层四角还建有突出楼体的"燕子窝"，可对碉楼四周形成上下左右全方位的控制。碉楼顶层多设有瞭望台，并配备了枪械、发电机、警报器、探照灯、石块以及铜锣等防卫装置。窗户比其他民居的窗户要小得多，都装有栅栏和窗扇，外设铁板窗门。大门则以厚重的钢板做成，一旦关上窗户和大门，碉楼就成了密闭的"保险柜"，刀枪不入。从这些特点也可以看出开平碉楼当时的防御功能。当然，在不同的历史时期，碉楼也发挥了不同的作用。在20世纪二三十年代，开平碉楼被用作中国共产党的地下活动场所，抗日战争后期成为抗日据点。

接下来就让我们走进自力村碉楼，感受那份历史的厚重与文化的韵味吧！

【自力村碉楼群】

自力村碉楼群位于开平市塘口镇。自力村由安和里、合安里、永安里三条方姓自然村组成，新中国成立初期，三村合称自力村，取"自力更生"之意。*速记 三安合称，自力更生。

自力村碉楼多建于20世纪二三十年代，为中西合璧的多层塔楼式建筑，是当地侨胞为保护家乡亲人的生命财产安全而兴建的。现存碉楼和庐共15座，它们是开平碉楼兴盛时期的杰出代表。

自力村碉楼的楼身高大，多为四到五层，门窗均为铁制，具备较强的防盗功能。墙体结构有钢筋混凝土的，也有混凝土包青砖的。建筑材料除青砖是本地产的外，铁枝、铁板、水泥等均是从外国进口的。

自力村的碉楼类型有更楼、众楼和居庐。除更楼外，其他碉楼建筑沿袭了当地传统建筑的"三间两廊"风格。这些建筑窗户狭小，外有进口的厚钢板，内有粗大的铁栅栏，最里一层才是玻璃窗。楼顶层的四角有一个凸出来的半圆形角堡，俗称"燕子窝"，其底部布有小孔，可以窥视楼下。

【铭石楼】

我们现在看到的这座碉楼是铭石楼，建于1925年，楼高6层，为钢筋混凝土结构，建筑材料中除了青砖是国产的以外，铁枝、铁板、水泥等都是从外国进口的。铭石楼的外形壮观，内部装饰豪华，充满了浓郁的欧洲风情。它的主人方润文是自力村人，早年远赴美国谋生，后来回国修建了这座碉楼。现在楼内完整地保存着当年的家具、生活设施、生产用具和日常生活用品，尤其是收藏至今的华侨书信、账簿、侨汇单据、老照片等文献资料，不仅见证了当年的乡村文化生活，更是研究华侨史的珍贵资料。铭石楼已经成为自力村碉楼群中的标志性建筑。

【方氏灯楼】

在这里，除了铭石楼，还有一座更楼值得大家打卡，那就是方氏灯楼，它是开平最具代表性的更楼。

方氏灯楼建于民国九年，也就是1920年，由今天的宅群、强亚两个村的方氏家族共同集资兴建，当时以方氏家族聚居的古宅地名和流经楼旁的一条小溪而命名为"古溪楼"。灯楼高18.43米，钢筋混凝土结构，共五层，标准层高三层，第四层为柱廊结构，四面悬挑，第五层是一个顶部像圆锅倒盖的亭子。建造这座更楼的目的主要是防备土匪。因为在20世纪二三十年代，马冈土塘一带的土匪四处烧杀抢掠，无恶不作。村民们经过商议，决定通过村民和海外侨胞集资的方式建造一座坚固的更楼。由于大家齐心协力，资金到位迅速，仅用八个月就建成了。方氏灯楼里面配备了发电机、探照灯和枪支弹药等，在当时为方氏家族防备土匪袭击起到了积极的预警、防备作用。

【结束语】

朋友们，如今我们处于高质量发展新时代，开平碉楼早已失去了当年的作用，但这些建筑充分体现了中国乡村民众面对外国先进文化时的一种自信、开放、包容的心态，也成为开平侨胞们留置于故土的一片精神守望地。

我的讲解到此结束，感谢大家的聆听！

三、英文讲解词示例

Kaiping Diaolou and Villages—Diaolou Clusters in Zili Village

Dear visitors, welcome to Kaiping, the beautiful hometown of overseas Chinese and Diaolou. Today let's visit Kaiping Diaolou.

Located in Kaiping, Jiangmen City of Guangdong Province, Diaolous were built at the beginning of the Qing Dynasty and mushroomed during the 1920s and 1930s. The number peaked at over 3300. Currently, there are 1833 Diaolous found in general investigation and registered in Kaiping. They serve as defense positions and residential buildings as well. These watchtowers represent a fusion between Chinese and Western architectural styles and are extolled as "classical works of overseas Chinese culture". On June 28, 2007, Kaiping Diaolou entered the World Cultural Heritage List by the UNESCO, being the first world cultural heritage in Guangdong Province.

Why the local people built Diaolou? The first reason is geographical conditon. As a low-lying place, Kaiping's territory is dominated by plains and subject to threats of typhoons and floods. The second reason is social factor. At the end of the Qing Dynasty and the beginning of the Republic of China, people suffered from social turmoil and local bandits. As a result, the local people built these defensive towers to protect their lives and property.

Varied in shapes, Diaolous combine multiple styles of ancient Greek, Rome and Islam. Buildings were built of four types: stone, rammed earth, bricks and concrete. Classified by function, these buildings take three forms: communal towers jointly built by several families, residential towers built by individual rich families, and watch towers for sounding the night watches and standing sentry.

Despite that different Diaolous are varied in building materials and styles, they have a lot in common: tall towers, thick walls, small doors and windows. Diaolous usually have several stories and are much taller than normal residential houses. So they allow residents to defend themselves from the top of the buildings. Walls are thicker and more solid than those of normal houses, protecting buildings from bandits crashing or setting fire. On the top floor, Diaolous have a bulgy, nest-liked balcony at each corner for thorough surveillance and defense of the whole building. Here you can also see defensive facilities like lookout towers, guns, power generators, alarms, searchlight, stones and gongs. Windows are much smaller, equipped with iron bars and panels. When closing those iron-barred windows and heavy steel doors, the building will be as secured as a "safe box". Not even a single bullet can be pumped into. Diaolous played a different role during the 1920s and the 1930s, serving as a venue for underground activities of members of the Communist Party of China (CPC). From 1937 to 1945, Diaolous became strongholds during the War of Resistance against Japan.

Now let's walk into the Diaolous in Zili Village to learn the piece of history and appreciate the culture!

Located in Tangkou Town of Kaiping, Zili Village is comprised of Anhe Lane, He'an Lane and Yong'an Lane. All the local villagers in these three natural villages have the same family name "Fang". After the founding of the People's Republic of China, three areas shared the same name "Zili Village". In Chinese, "Zili" means "self-dependence".

Most of the Diaolous in Zili Village were built in the 1920s or the 1930s. Those multi-storied buildings show a unity between Chinese and Western architectural styles. They were built by local overseas Chinese to protect lives and properties of families and villagers. There are 15 existing Diaolous and residential towers. All of them are perfect examples of Kaiping Diaolou in golden era.

Diaolous in this village are tall and giant. Most of them are four- or five-storied. The doors and windows are made of iron. Walls are usually made of reinforced concrete, some concrete plus blue bricks. Blue bricks were locally produced while iron bars, iron panels and cement were imported.

The Diaolous in this village take three forms: watch towers, communal towers and residential towers. Except for watch towers, other buildings follow the traditional architectural style: three rooms in a row and corridors at both the front and back. This type of building has narrow windows. They are covered by imported heavy steel panels, guarded by thick iron bars in between and protected by glass screens inside. There is a bulgy, semicircle, nest-liked balcony called "bird's nest" at each corner of the top floor. Holes can be found on the floor of each balcony, which allows residents to watch over what was happening below.

Now we are standing in front of the Mingshi Hall. Established in 1925, the 6-storied tower is built of reinforced concrete. In terms of building materials, blue bricks were produced at home while iron bars, iron panels and cement were imported from foreign countries. The magnificent building with luxurious interior design shows a rich and flamboyant European style. Fang Runwen, the owner of the Mingshi Hall, was a local villager. He went to the US to make a living at an early age. After he made a fortune, he returned to build this hall. Inside the hall, furniture, living facilities, production tools, daily life necessities and even some valuable materials such as letters written by overseas Chinese, account books, overseas remittance, and old pictures still remain intact. All these things not only reflect the local cultural life in rural areas at that time, but also provide good opportunities to learn the history of overseas Chinese. The Mingshi Hall has become a landmark building of Zili Village.

Dear friends, right now we are in a new era of high-quality development, Diaolous were no longer put into use for defense. But these buildings fully reflect Chinese villagers' confidence, tolerance and inclusiveness when facing advanced foreign culture. Diaolous have become a spiritual watchtower left by the overseas Chinese.

That's the end of my tour guide commentary. Thank you for listening!

四、综合知识

☆开平碉楼是中国乡土建筑的一个特殊类型，是集防卫、居住和中西建筑艺术于一体的多层塔楼式建筑，被誉为"华侨文化的典范之作""令人震撼的建筑艺术长廊""世界建筑艺术博物馆"。

☆2001年，开平碉楼作为近现代重要史迹及代表性建筑，被国务院批准列入第五批全国重点文物保护单位。2007年，被联合国教科文组织列入世界遗产名录，是广东省首个世界文化遗产。

☆开平碉楼始建于清初，而兴建则主要集中在20世纪二三十年代，在鼎盛时期达3300多座。目前，经开平市人民政府普查、登记在册的有1833座。开平碉楼与村落共包括4个遗产片区：赤坎镇三门里迎龙楼、塘口镇自力村村落与方氏灯楼、百合镇马降龙村落、蚬冈镇锦江里村落。

☆开平市是著名的华侨之乡、建筑之乡和艺术之乡。地处珠江三角洲西南部，毗邻香港、澳门，旅居海外的华侨和港澳台同胞75万，遍布世界67个国家和地区，故有"海内海外两开平"之说。早在16世纪中叶，就有开平人到南洋地区谋生，但大规模的移民和侨乡的形成源于19世纪中叶掀起的海外移民运动。这些华侨华人在稍有积蓄后便汇款回乡买田建房，兴办实业，开平碉楼的建设在20世纪30年代达到高峰。

☆赤坎镇三门里村内的迎龙楼，以其为开平市现存最早的碉楼、形制最原始而著称；塘口镇自力村村落以碉楼相对集中而闻名，方氏灯楼是开平最具代表性的更楼，原名"古溪楼"；百合镇马降龙村落被誉为"世界上最美的碉楼村落"，以天禄楼最具代表性；而蚬冈镇锦江里村内的瑞石楼，是开平现存最高、最精美、最豪华的碉楼，有"开平第一楼"之称。

☆广大侨胞为了防洪防匪，保护侨眷安全，纷纷兴建居守兼备的碉楼。从地区分布上看，华侨、港澳同胞比较多，盗匪频发的地方，碉楼分布比较多，特别是塘口、赤坎两镇，每村少则一座，多则十多座。

☆按功能分，开平碉楼有用作家族居住的居庐、村人共同集资兴建的众楼以及主要用于打更放哨的更楼。从建筑款式上看，有中国传统式的、中西合璧的，还有古希腊、古罗马及伊斯兰等风格的；有别墅式的、庭院式的，还有教堂式的，较为全面地融汇了世界各国建筑的精华。

☆从建筑材料上看，开平碉楼分为石楼、夯土楼、砖楼和钢筋混凝土楼（含砖混楼）。其中砖楼所用的砖有三种：一是明朝土法烧制的红砖，二是清朝和民国时期当地烧制的青砖，三是近代的红砖。钢筋混凝土楼主要分布在平原和丘陵地区，多建于20世纪二三十年代，是华侨吸取世界各国建筑不同特点设计建造的，造型最能体现中西合璧的建筑特色。

☆门窗窄小、铁门铁窗，墙身厚实，墙体设置枪眼是开平碉楼的共同特点。枪眼大体上都开成长方形或"T"字形。大多数碉楼在接近楼顶的两层建有阔于楼体的平台，并筑有走廊，楼顶配建各式凉亭，或在四个角筑有突出楼体的"燕子窝"。这样的设计，既利于在楼上自由活动，又利于观察周围远近的动静，还可以从平台或"燕子窝"的枪眼中，居高临下对碉楼的上下左右进行全方位的控制。碉楼顶层一般设有瞭望台，不少设有火药炮、铜钟、报警器、发电机、探照灯等防患设施。

☆抗日战争时期，开平碉楼还发挥了抗击日本侵略者的作用。如著名的"南楼七烈士"事件。南楼，是赤坎镇腾蛟村一座建成于1913年的碉楼，楼高19米，共7层，位于水陆交通要塞，地形险要。1945年7月16日，日军分兵三路进犯赤坎，并于次日晚进攻南楼，驻守南楼的司徒四乡自卫队凭楼抵抗到7月25日，最终司徒煦等七名壮士被俘。他们面对敌人的严刑拷打宁死不屈，次日壮烈牺牲。现在南楼已成为开平市著名的爱国主义教育基地。

☆自力村碉楼现存15座，风格各异，造型精美，是开平碉楼兴盛时期的杰出代表，多建于20世纪二三十年代，是当地侨胞为保护家乡亲人的生命财产安全而兴建的。这些碉楼均铁门、铁窗，遍布射击孔，配备了枪械、铜锣、探照灯，并储存了大量的粮食。墙体的结构有钢筋混凝土的，也有混凝土包青砖的。建筑材料除青砖是本地出产外，铁枝、铁板、水泥等均从外国进口。建筑风格上，很多带有外国的建筑特色，有柱廊式、平台式、城堡式的，也有混合式的。2005年11月，自力村被评为"全国历史文化名村"。

江门市开平碉楼与村落

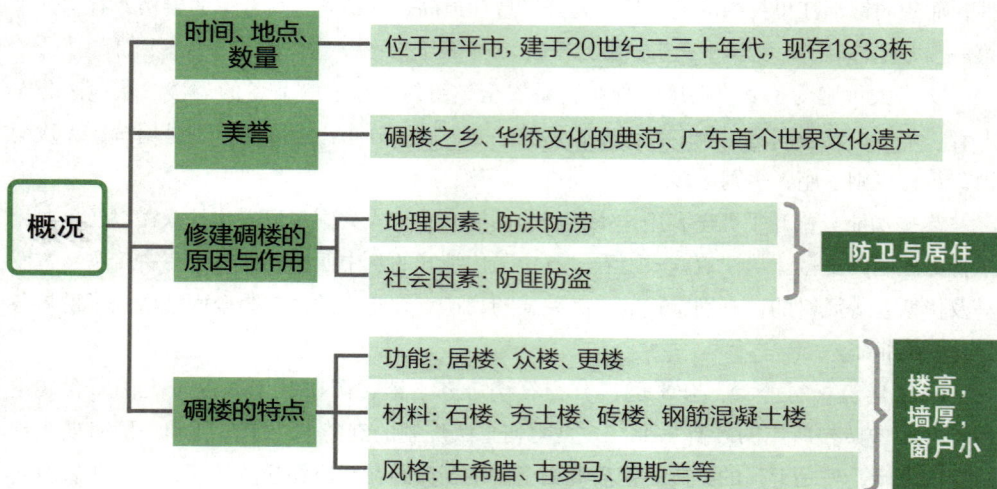

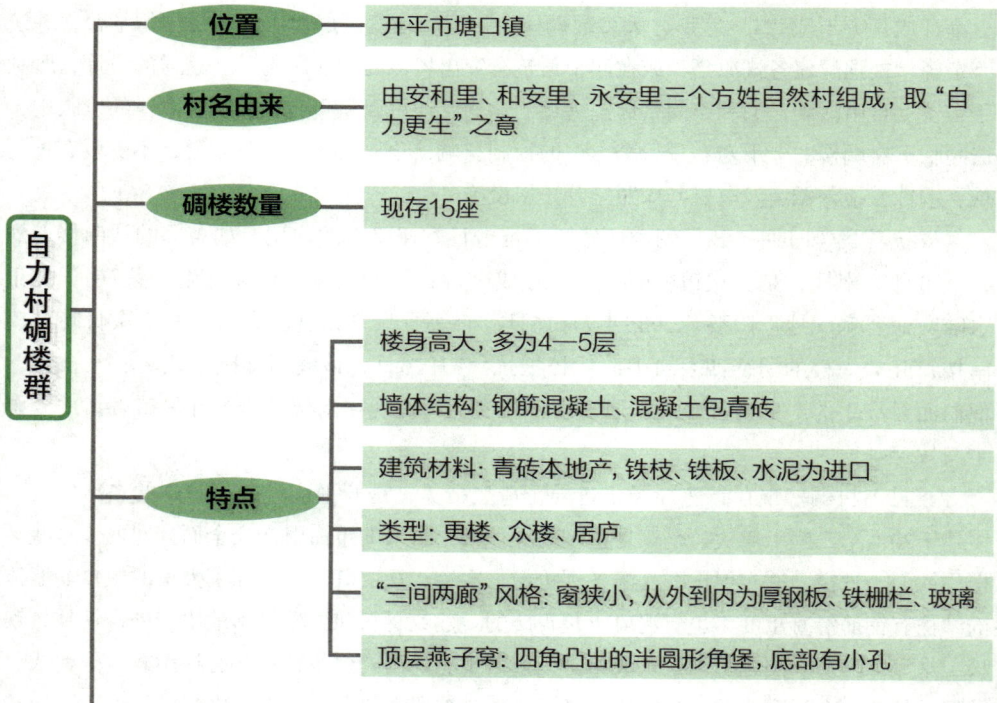

概况

时间、地点、数量
位于开平市，建于20世纪二三十年代，现存1833栋

美誉
碉楼之乡、华侨文化的典范、广东首个世界文化遗产

修建碉楼的原因与作用
- 地理因素：防洪防涝
- 社会因素：防匪防盗

防卫与居住

碉楼的特点
- 功能：居楼、众楼、更楼
- 材料：石楼、夯土楼、砖楼、钢筋混凝土楼
- 风格：古希腊、古罗马、伊斯兰等

楼高，墙厚，窗户小

自力村碉楼群

位置
开平市塘口镇

村名由来
由安和里、和安里、永安里三个方姓自然村组成，取"自力更生"之意

碉楼数量
现存15座

特点
- 楼身高大，多为4—5层
- 墙体结构：钢筋混凝土、混凝土包青砖
- 建筑材料：青砖本地产，铁枝、铁板、水泥为进口
- 类型：更楼、众楼、居庐
- "三间两廊"风格：窗狭小，从外到内为厚钢板、铁栅栏、玻璃
- 顶层燕子窝：四角凸出的半圆形角堡，底部有小孔

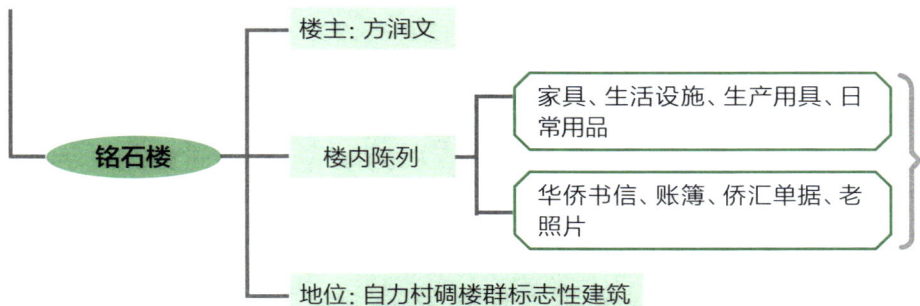

- 铭石楼
  - 楼主：方润文
  - 楼内陈列
    - 家具、生活设施、生产用具、日常用品
    - 华侨书信、账簿、侨汇单据、老照片
  - 地位：自力村碉楼群标志性建筑

乡村文化＋华侨文化

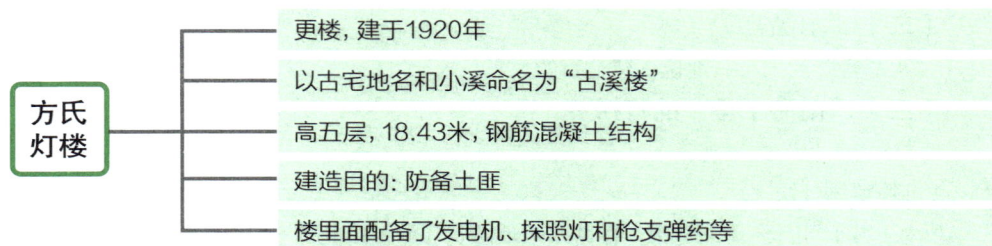

- 方氏灯楼
  - 更楼，建于1920年
  - 以古宅地名和小溪命名为"古溪楼"
  - 高五层，18.43米，钢筋混凝土结构
  - 建造目的：防备土匪
  - 楼里面配备了发电机、探照灯和枪支弹药等

第十节 阳江市广东海上丝绸之路博物馆景区

一、讲解要点

（一）概述

1.海上丝绸之路博物馆的地理位置、面积、建筑特色。

2.海上丝绸之路博物馆的主题、别称、美誉。

（二）"水晶宫"

"水晶宫"的大小、地位、建造目的。

（三）"南海Ⅰ号"的打捞

1."南海Ⅰ号"的发现。

2.沉箱整体打捞法。

3."南海Ⅰ号"的出水文物：瓷器、木爪碇石、船员用品等。

二、中文讲解词示例

【欢迎词】

大家好！欢迎来到广东海上丝绸之路博物馆参观。

【概述】

广东海上丝绸之路博物馆，简称"海丝馆"，位于广东省阳江市海陵岛十里银滩。海丝馆建筑面积近2万平方米，主馆占地面积约1.2万平方米，建筑设计融合了海洋和岭南文化的元素，在造型上把古代造船的龙骨结构和岭南地区的干栏式建筑结合起来。建筑的外立面由五个大小不一的椭圆体连环相扣组成，看起来既像大海起伏的波浪，又似展翅飞翔的海鸥。整个建筑体现了海洋文化与南方建筑风格的优美组合。

海丝馆因宋代古沉船"南海Ⅰ号"整体打捞出水而建，以古沉船的发掘、保护、展示与研究为主题，是世界著名的沉船博物馆，更是中国水下考古的里程碑，因此海丝馆又被称为"南海Ⅰ号"博物馆。海丝馆被评为国家一级博物馆、国家5A级旅游景区。敦煌莫高窟拥有将近5万幅壁画和6万多件文物，而海丝馆出水文物达18万余件，远远超过了敦煌莫高窟的文物数量，因此海丝馆还享有"海上敦煌"的美誉。*速记 1（一级博物馆）5（5A级旅游景区）18（18万件文物）。

现在，就请大家跟随我去深入了解"南海Ⅰ号"的前世今生以及出水文物。馆内展览有常设展"南海Ⅰ号"基本陈列，将"南海Ⅰ号"的前世今生与海上丝绸之路的文化相结合，讲述了"南海Ⅰ号"的整体打捞过程，展示了精美的出水文物，再现了宋代海外贸易的繁荣景象。*提示 馆内基本陈列共分为七个展厅：扬帆、沉没、探秘、出水、价值、遗珍、成果。可按照展厅顺序进行讲解。

【"水晶宫"】

南宋初年，一艘通过海上丝绸之路向外运送瓷器的木船失事沉没于今天广东阳江对开的南海海域，1987年被发现并命名为"南海Ⅰ号"。这艘船在海底沉睡800多年后，2007年底被整体打捞上岸并成功移放海丝馆的"水晶宫"。

我们现在看到的中间最大的椭圆体即是为"南海Ⅰ号"沉船量身定做的家园，它南北长60米，东西长40米，水深12米，其水体容量达到3万立方米，是世界最大的室内水体，因而整个建筑被形象地称为"水晶宫"。为了保持文物发现时的原貌，"水晶宫"里的水质和温度等都保持与"南海Ⅰ号"出水时所在的海底环境完全一样。透过透明玻璃，可以看到"南海Ⅰ号"船体表面还覆盖着一层厚厚的海底淤泥，也能看到打捞时装载"南海Ⅰ号"的沉箱。

【打捞"南海Ⅰ号"】

"南海Ⅰ号"船长30.4米，残存约22米，船宽约9米，是目前我国发现年代较早、体量巨大、保存相对完整的古代远洋贸易商船。大家可能会好奇，"南海Ⅰ号"是如何打捞上岸，又是怎样移到"水晶宫"的。这得从1987年发现"南海Ⅰ号"古沉船后说起。发现古沉船后我国成立了水下考古机构，当时用传统的水下考古方法，除了打捞沉船上的文物之外无法完成对古沉船的测绘、摄影等工作，这将会损失很多宝贵的信息。直到2003年，广州打捞局提出了整体打捞的概念，经过三年反复论证，2007年决定正式实施整体打捞行动。"南海Ⅰ号"的整体打捞法，通俗地讲就是制作一个尺寸大于沉船的箱子沉入海底，完全罩住沉船，然后在海底为沉箱安装好箱底，将沉船以及沉船上的淤泥和海水一起装入沉箱，再用最大吊力达4000吨的巨型起重船"华天龙"号将沉箱和沉船一起打捞出水，通过半潜船的配合作业将装载沉船的沉箱拉移到海丝馆进行保存和保护。采用沉箱整体打捞的方法，在世界范围内是一个首创性的工作，体现了我国打捞行业的创新精神。

【出水文物】

"南海Ⅰ号"船载文物有数十万件。目前考古发掘出水的文物精品达18万余件，主要是瓷器、金银器、铁器、漆器、动植物残骸、植物果核等。尤其以瓷器居多，瓷器主要有江西景德镇窑、浙江龙泉窑、福建德化窑、磁灶窑、闽清义窑等。现在我们看到的展柜中的文物都是"南海Ⅰ号"出水的精美瓷器。*提示 瓷器品种尽量记，能记几个记几个。

这是木爪碇石，木爪碇石由雕凿成条状的"碇石"与木质的"爪子"箍扎合成，跟现代船锚的作用一样。

这里展示的是"南海Ⅰ号"上船员的生活用品，有玉雕罗汉、铜镜、木梳、墨砚、朱砂等，我们可以通过这些文物了解当年船员们在海上的生活场景。

【结束语】

我的讲解到此结束了，接下来的时间留给大家自由参观，谢谢大家的支持和配合！

三、英文讲解词示例

Maritime Silk Road Museum of Guangdong in Yangjiang City

Welcome to Maritime Silk Road Museum of Guangdong.

Maritime Silk Road Museum of Guangdong is located at Shili Silver Beach, Hailing Island of Yangjiang City. The museum has an area of nearly 20,000 square meters. The main hall has a size of 12,000 square meters. The architectural design combines elements of ocean and Lingnan culture. In terms of interior design, the designer combines elements of keel of ancient ship and stilt style houses in Lingnan area. The facade is comprised of five ovals of different sizes. All of them are connected with each other. The whole pattern looks like undulant waves or a flying seagull. The whole building shows a perfect fusion of maritime culture and architectural style in south China.

Maritime Silk Road Museum of Guangdong was built with an aim to protect, exhibit and research Nanhai No.1, an ancient shipwreck in the Song Dynasty. As a famous shipwreck-themed museum, it is also a milestone of underwater archaeology in China. That's why the museum is also called "Nanhai No.1 Museum". It is rated as a National First-Level Museum and National 5A Scenic Area. The museum is extolled as "Maritime Dunhuang" because it has over 180,000 cultural relics, much more than those in Mogao Caves in Dunhuang.

Now let's walk into the museum to learn the history of the Nanhai No.1 and appreciate its exquisite cultural relics. There is a permanent exhibition with the theme of the Nanhai No.1. It shows both the history of the shipwreck and culture of the Maritime Silk Road. You can learn the whole process of salvage operation, appreciate those beautiful cultural relics and admire booming foreign trade in the Song Dynasty.

At the beginning of the Southern Song Dynasty, a wooden ship carrying ceramics unfortunately had an accident and sank in the South China Sea near Yangjiang. The ship was discovered in 1987 and named "Nanhai No.1". Lying at the bottom of the sea for more than 800 years, the whole ship was salvaged successfully at the end of 2007 and displayed in the "Crystal Palace" of the museum.

The largest oval in the middle is the area specifically designed for the Nanhai No.1. The place is 60 meters long from north to south and 40 meters wide from east to west. It has the world's largest indoor water body with a depth of 12 meters, and a total volume of 30,000 cubic meters. As a result, the whole building has another vivid name called the "Crystal Palace". In order to keep the original appearance of the ship, we replicate the sea environment in which the sunken ship was discovered. Looking through the transparent glass screen, we can see the shipwreck was covered by thick sludge. We can also see a caisson used to carry the shipwreck in salvage.

The original Nanhai No.1 was 30.4 meters long. The shipwreck is about 22 meters long and 9 meters wide. So far, it is the biggest and relatively complete ancient merchant ship with the longest history discovered in China. Some of you might wonder how the Nanhai No.1 was excavated and moved to the Crystal Palace. Back to 1987, the ancient merchant ship was found in the South China Sea. After that, an underwater archaeological organization was officially established. Archaeologists thought that even though traditional underwater archaeological methods could allow them to salvaged cultural relics on the shipwreck, they could not finish drafting and photographing of it. That would surely lead to a great loss of valuable information. In 2003, Guangzhou Salvage Bureau of the Ministry of Transport finally put forward a plan for excavation of the whole ship. After three years' thorough and careful analysis, the implementation of the plan was finally started in 2007. A caisson bigger than the underwater shipwreck was made and sunk into the sea in order to completely cover it. Then a caisson base was installed under the water so that the sunken ship, sludge and even seawater were all contained in the caisson. All of them were excavated out of the water by a giant pontoon crane named "Huatian Dragon", which has 4000 tons of lifting force. After that, a semi-submerged ship was operated to deliver the caisson and shipwreck to the museum for protection. The whole salvage operation was a groundbreaking work in the world. It reflects the Chinese people's pioneering spirit in archaeological excavation.

The Nanhai No.1 carried several hundred thousand cultural relics. 180,000 of them were found in archaeological excavation, including ceramics, gold, silver, copper and iron relics, lacquer wares, animals and plants remains and fruit pits. Most of them are ceramics from Jiangxi Jingdezhen Kiln, Zhejiang Longquan Kiln, Dehua Kiln, Cizao Kiln and Minqingyi Kiln in Fujian. Now we can see those beautiful ceramics from the Nanhai No.1.

This is called "Dingshi", which looks like a papaya. The papaya-shaped Dingshi is made up of stone bar and a wooden claw-like object. It serves as an anchor on of a modern ship.

Here you can see exhibition of daily necessities of sailors on the ship, including jade arhat sculptures, bronze mirrors, wooden combs, ink stones, cinnabar, and so on. All these exhibits enable us to learn how sailors lived and work on the ship.

That's the end of my tour commentary. Now it's time for you to enjoy the exhibition freely. Thank you for your cooperation.

四、综合知识

☆海上丝绸之路博物馆展出的"南海Ⅰ号"上打捞出水的相关文物达18万余件，有瓷器、石雕、朱砂、木梳、铜环等；还展出了许多阳江本土文物，既有新石器时期的石制工具、战国时期的青铜器、东汉时期的彩陶马头和铜鼓等，也有唐代素三彩小杯、清代银质饰物等。

☆ "南海Ⅰ号"出水的瓷器包括了江西景德镇窑，福建德化窑、磁灶窑等窑口的产品，许多瓷器带有异域风格，如德化窑的仿金银器执壶。大量的瓷器沉没在海面下20米深处，被1至2米厚的淤泥所覆盖，天然密封的环境，在一定程度上阻隔了海水和海底微生物的腐蚀。

☆ "南海Ⅰ号"已陆续出水铜钱数万枚。其中，年代最早的是汉代的五铢钱，最晚的是南宋赵构时期的"绍兴元宝"。

☆ "南海Ⅰ号"出水的金器中，有一条金腰带，打捞于1987年。腰带全长1.72米，仍金光闪耀。腰带工艺精良，带体呈麻花状，带扣装饰细腻浮点状纹饰，极具异域风情。专家推测该腰带为中东地区器物样式，是海上丝绸之路的又一实物见证。

☆ "南海Ⅰ号"是一艘南宋时期的木质古沉船，于1987年被广州救捞局与英国海洋探测公司在距阳江市海陵岛30多海里的海区意外发现。2007年12月22日，"南海Ⅰ号"以整体打捞的方式成功出水，用沉箱整体打捞"南海Ⅰ号"古船的方案是史无前例的，开启了中国水下考古先河，是中国水下考古事业的重要里程碑。"南海Ⅰ号"的打捞已经作为联合国教科文组织推荐的经典案例向全球推广，成为中国水下考古界的骄傲。

☆考古专家从船体结构、船型工艺等方面判断，"南海Ⅰ号"属于"福船"类型。福船，是福建沿海所造木帆船的统称，与广船、沙船、浙船并称中国四大船型，也是中国古代海船的主要船型。

☆ "南海Ⅰ号"所用木材产自中国东南沿海、西南及南亚等地区，因此可判定该船为中国制造。据推测，"南海Ⅰ号"的始发港为当时的贸易港口泉州港，可能曾停靠广州港等地。

☆ "南海Ⅰ号"上打捞出水的木爪碇石由木质的"爪"和碇石两部分组成。其中，碇石长3.1米，重840多斤，花岗岩质，菱形，是目前为止发现的形体最大、最重的宋代碇石。古代造船中，船的长度大约为碇石长度的10倍，可据此推算"南海Ⅰ号"完整长度为31米左右。

☆用沉箱的方法打捞"南海Ⅰ号"的方案中，最难的是吊放沉箱环节。沉箱有33米长、14米宽、500多吨重，分上下两层。水下定位难度非常大，沉箱放下去以后几乎无法再调整位置，必须一次放准。

☆ "南海Ⅰ号"底舱装的都是相对较轻的物体，船体下轻上重；而当时的许多外国船的底舱装满石头，船体下重上轻，稳定性更高。这是因为中国船主要运输瓷器，如果船体下重上轻，虽然稳定性提高了，但摇摆周期变快，会加剧瓷器在运输过程中的相互碰撞，提高瓷器的货损率，不利于海外贸易。

☆ "南海Ⅰ号"装载了不少金属制造的商品，如铜环、铜珠等。有些制品只经过了初步的铸造或打磨，如铜环等表面并无花纹等装饰的痕迹，据推测可能是中国制造的半成品，通过"南海Ⅰ号"运往海外进行深加工。

☆随"南海Ⅰ号"出水的青白釉刻划花卉纹葵口碗，属花瓣形，浅腹，圈足，施青白釉，釉色莹润，内壁有五道花瓣纹为饰。造型精致，是义窑的代表之作。义窑位于福州市闽清县东桥镇义窑村一带，是一处规模宏大、具有地方特色的著名民窑。义窑主烧青白釉瓷，以日用粗器为主，产品器类丰富，有碗、洗、盅、壶、盒、钵、盅、炉和动物雕塑等。

☆随"南海Ⅰ号"出水的德化窑陶瓷有青白釉三联杯印花子母盒、青白釉印牡丹纹六棱带盖执壶、青白釉印花卉纹八棱盒等。德化窑位于福建德化县，是福建沿海地区古代外销瓷重要产地之一，瓷器大量外销至东亚、东南亚乃至非洲。

☆随"南海Ⅰ号"出水的景德镇窑陶瓷有青白釉印缠枝花卉纹折沿芒口盘、青白釉印花出筋菊瓣纹斗笠盏、青白釉碗等。景德镇窑是中国最重要的瓷窑之一，在今江西景德镇，在宋代以烧制青白瓷为主。景德镇窑青白瓷对江南地区瓷窑影响很大，形成了一个以景德镇为中心的青白瓷系，是江南地区两大瓷窑系之一，居宋代六大瓷系之首。

☆随"南海Ⅰ号"出水了一批"喇叭口"大瓷碗，为德化窑所产。这些瓷碗器形较大，类似阿拉伯人手抓饭使用的喇叭口瓷盘，可能是专门的外销瓷。据宋代《诸蕃志》记载，东南亚一些国家"饮食以葵叶为碗，不施匙筋，掬而食之"，多以植物叶子为食器。中国陶瓷输入以后，提供了精美实用的器皿。印度尼西亚国家博物馆展出了大量瓷器文物，其中就有德化窑"喇叭口"大瓷碗。

☆宋代，一些海外商人根据自己的审美和喜好，要求中国工人按照其给出的图纸或实物进行仿制加工。"南海Ⅰ号"除了中国特色的常见器物外，也出水了很多明显带有异域风格的器物，比如西亚、阿拉伯风格的六棱执壶，可能就是根据国外市场要求定制的。

阳江市广东海上丝绸之路博物馆景区

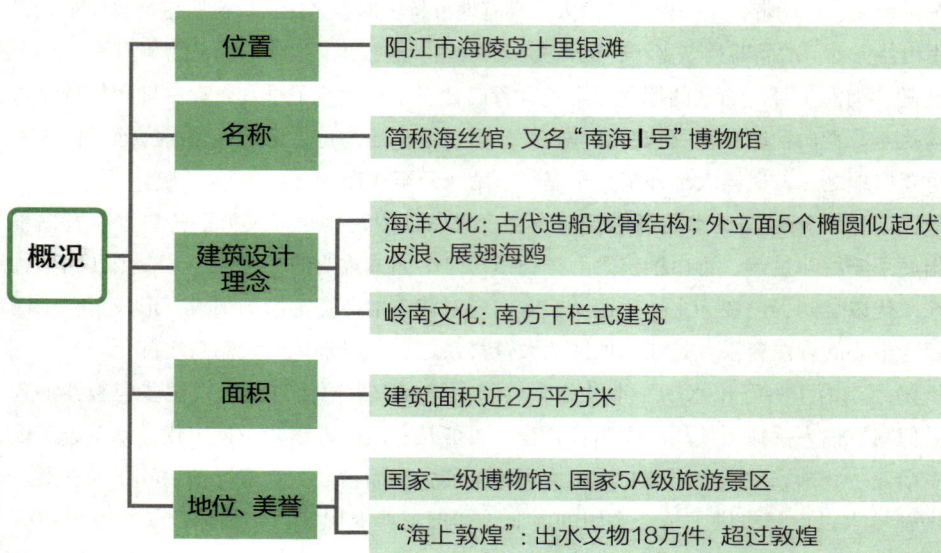

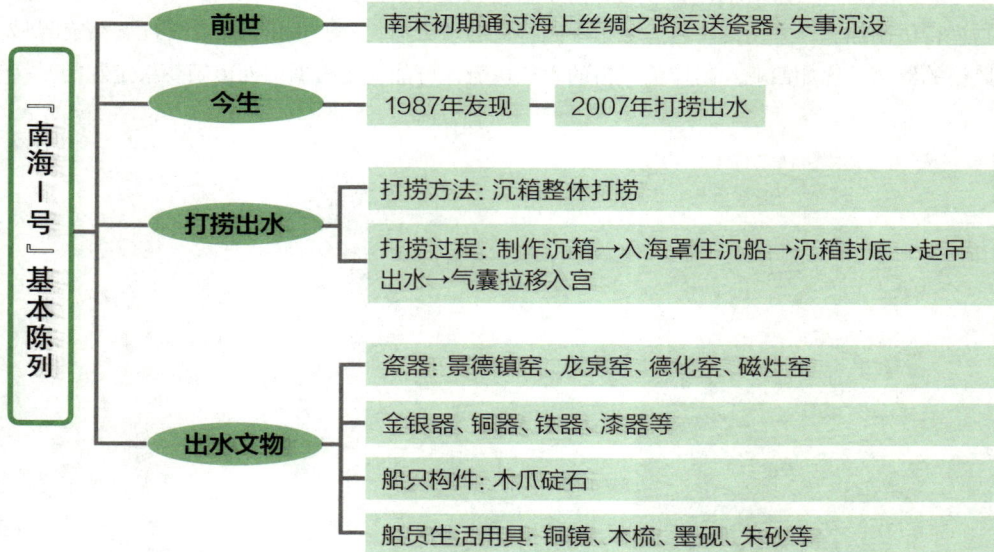

概况
- **位置** —— 阳江市海陵岛十里银滩
- **名称** —— 简称海丝馆，又名"南海 I 号"博物馆
- **建筑设计理念**
  - 海洋文化: 古代造船龙骨结构; 外立面5个椭圆似起伏波浪、展翅海鸥
  - 岭南文化: 南方干栏式建筑
- **面积** —— 建筑面积近2万平方米
- **地位、美誉**
  - 国家一级博物馆、国家5A级旅游景区
  - "海上敦煌": 出水文物18万件, 超过敦煌

『南海 I 号』基本陈列
- **前世** —— 南宋初期通过海上丝绸之路运送瓷器, 失事沉没
- **今生** —— 1987年发现 —— 2007年打捞出水
- **打捞出水**
  - 打捞方法: 沉箱整体打捞
  - 打捞过程: 制作沉箱→入海罩住沉船→沉箱封底→起吊出水→气囊拉移入宫
- **出水文物**
  - 瓷器: 景德镇窑、龙泉窑、德化窑、磁灶窑
  - 金银器、铜器、铁器、漆器等
  - 船只构件: 木爪碇石
  - 船员生活用具: 铜镜、木梳、墨砚、朱砂等

第十一节　肇庆市七星岩风景区

一、讲解要点

（一）概述

1.七星岩的面积和主要景观。

2.七星岩名字的由来、叶剑英元帅的诗篇。

（二）七星岩摩崖石刻

1.摩崖石刻的含义。

2.七星岩摩崖石刻的规模、特点和地位。

3.七星岩摩崖石刻代表作：李邕的《端州石室记》。

（三）龙岩洞

1.龙岩洞的组成。

2.龙岩洞内的景观。

3.钟乳石的成因。

二、中文讲解词示例

【欢迎词】

各位游客，大家好！欢迎来到被誉为"人间仙境""岭南第一奇观"的国家5A级旅游景区——肇庆七星岩风景区。

【概述】

七星岩景区总占地面积达8.23平方千米，以峰林、溶洞、湖泊、碑刻、寺观为主要景观。

七星岩景区历史悠久，从唐朝至今，游人络绎不绝，名人纷至沓来，留下了众多碑刻墨宝。尽管唐代已有游迹，但七星岩这个名字是从北宋才开始有的。为什么叫七星岩呢？肇庆一带为喀斯特地貌，岩层极易被流水侵蚀，肇庆湿热多雨，慢慢便把岩石侵蚀成峰林石山，这便是七星岩的峰林地貌。阆风岩、玉屏岩、石室岩、天柱岩、蟾蜍岩、仙掌岩、阿坡岩七座石灰岩山峰，形似北斗七星般排列在碧波如镜、近6.49万平方千米的星湖上，20多千米的林荫湖堤，如绿色飘带般把仙女湖、中心湖、波海湖、青莲湖和里湖连结在一起，湖光山色，绰约多姿。

叶剑英元帅在游览后曾赋诗一首："借得西湖水一圜，更移阳朔七堆山。堤边添上丝丝柳，画幅长留天地间。"高度赞扬了七星岩独一无二的美景。还有人这样评价七星岩："五岳归来不看山，料应未上七星岩。"

【摩崖石刻】

接下来，大家继续跟我往前走。在我们眼前的就是摩崖石刻群。什么是"摩崖石刻"呢？中国人自古习惯把刻有图文的方形石板称为"碑"，圆形的则称为"碣"；对于镌刻在天然岩石上的图文，则称为"摩崖石刻"，也简称为"摩崖"或者"石刻"。"摩崖石刻"起初是为了铭功和记事，后来也加入了选刻诗文、佛经、佛像等内容。

有人说，山是景区骨架，水是景区容颜，动植物是景区的点缀，而人文景观则是景区的灵魂。七星岩的摩崖石刻现有600多幅，它们分布密集，保存完整，文体齐全，字体纷繁，中外兼备，是我国南方保存数量最多、最集中、质量最高的一处摩崖石刻群，也是国家级重点文物保护单位。

这些石刻，集诗词歌赋、游记史实、对联题咏与崖刻画于一壁，故又有"千年诗廊"之美誉。它们不仅是精美的石刻艺术品，而且记述了肇庆的地理环境、山河变迁、历史大事、宗教信仰等，是研究我国唐朝以来各个朝代的政治、经济和文化发展历程的重要实物资料。*技巧 讲解时可穿插与游客的互动，比如让游客猜猜是哪位名人的手笔。

在七星岩摩崖石刻群中，年代最久远的要数李邕的《端州石室记》。其笔力遒劲，清丽端庄，是李邕传世的唯一正楷刻石，实属石刻中的瑰宝，素有"镇岩之宝"的美誉。它像初唐其他散文一样，沿袭汉魏六朝赋体骈文的句式，读起来抑扬顿挫，朗朗上口。可惜由于年代久远，有些字已残缺难辨了。宋朝时，这里又多了个马蹄形的损坏痕迹，所以后人称它为"马蹄碑"。《端州石室记》有三绝：文绝、字绝、雕刻绝。它的价值更在于它精湛的书法艺术。

【龙岩洞】

接下来，我们将深入探索七星岩核心景点之一的龙岩洞。龙岩洞作为七星岩中最具神秘色彩和观赏价值的溶洞之一，是七星岩溶洞群的重要组成部分，与碧霞洞和莲花洞共同构成了七星岩的溶洞奇观。龙岩洞以自然形成的钟乳石景观为主，洞内钟乳石形态各异，有的如飞瀑流泉，有的似仙山楼阁，让人仿佛置身于一个奇幻的地下宫殿之中。

在彩灯的映照下，形态各异的钟乳石、石笋、石幔错落有致，有的如飞瀑直下，有的似玉柱擎天，更有无数石花、石珊瑚点缀其间，让人目不暇接，叹为观止。

这些钟乳石是千万年来，雨水沿岩石缝隙不断渗入，溶解石灰岩，并在洞内结晶而成的。它们或悬挂于洞顶，或矗立于地面，形态万千，令人叹为观止。在这里，您可以欣赏到"五谷丰登""桃园三结义""狮子看骆驼""雄狮怒吼"等生动逼真的钟乳石景观，每一处都体现了大自然的神奇。*技巧 讲解自然景观时，除了描述其"象形"之外，还可以从科学角度科普成因，以增加讲解的知识性。

【结束语】

游客朋友们，请大家放慢脚步，细细品味大自然的恩赐，感受历史的厚重与文化的魅力吧！谢谢大家的聆听！

三、英文讲解词示例

Seven Star Crags of Zhaoqing

Hello, everyone! Welcome to the National 5A Scenic Area, the Seven Star Crags scenic area. It is also called "The Heaven on Earth", "The First Wonder in Lingnan Area".

Seven Star Crags scenic area covers 8.23 square kilometers. Peak forests, caves, lakes, inscriptions, and temples are key scenic spots.

Seven Star Crags has a long history as a scenic spot. Since the Tang dynasty, endless streams of tourists and celebrities visited this place and left a large number of inscriptions, calligraphy works and paintings. Seven Star Crags didn't get its name until the Northern Song Dynasty. So why Seven Star Crags? The topography of Zhaoqing is a karst landform. Rock layers are easily eroded by running water. Due to the humid and rainy weather, rocks were gradually eroded into peaks and hills, and formed peak forest landscape of Seven Star Crags. It consists of seven limestone hillocks, namely, Langfeng Rock, Jade Screen Rock, Stone Chamber Rock, Heavenly Pillar Rock, Toad Rock, Immortal Palm Rock and Apo Rock. Standing in the clear water of Xinghu, which means "Star Lake", of 64.9 thousand square kilometers in area, their layout resembles the constellation Big Dipper. The 20-km-long Xinghu Tour-lake Greenway links the Fairy Lake, the Central Lake, Bohai Lake, Lotus Lake and the Inner Lake, creating a picturesque scene.

Marshal Ye Jianying wrote a poem after his visit: "The water here is smooth like the pretty West Lake, the peaks here splendid like the amazing ones in Yangshuo. The causeways are dotted with graceful willows for beauty's sake, as if in fantastic pictures I rove." It highly praises the unique scenery of Seven Star Crags. Others also commented that "If one refuses mountains other than the Five Great Mountains of China, he should pay a visit to Seven Star Crags."

Now please follow me. Here in front of us is the cliff-side inscriptions. Why is it called the cliff-side inscriptions? In ancient times, the Chinese people called the square stone tablets engraved with pictures and texts as "Bei", which means steles, while the round ones are called "Jie", which means stone tablet. For the pictures and texts engraved on rocks in the nature, it is called cliff-side inscriptions. also known as "cliff inscription" or "stone carving". These cliff-side inscriptions were originally for inscription and memorization, and later also engraved poetry, Buddhist sutras, Buddhist status and others.

Some people say that, mountains are the backbone of scenic areas, water is the complexion of these spots, animals and plants are the decoration, and culture landscape is the soul. There are over 600 cliff-side inscriptions in Seven Star Crags. They are densely distributed and well-preserved, with a variety of styles and characters, both in Chinese and foreign languages. As one of the sites with most abundant, concentrated and high-quality inscription i in southern China, it is also one of the Major Historical and Cultural Site Protected at the National Level.

These carvings of poems, travelogue, history, antithetical couplets and cliff inscriptions are all depicted on the cliff. So it is also renowned as the "poetry gallery of a thousand years". They are more than beautiful carving works of art, but also documented geographical environment, changes in hills and rivers, historical events, religious beliefs, and other aspects of Zhaoqing. They are important materials for the study of the political, economic and cultural development of each dynasty since the Tang Dynasty in China.

Among the inscriptions of Seven Star Crags, the one with the longest history is *the Stories of Duanzhou Stone Chamber* by Li Yong. His calligraphy is featured with powerful strokes, looking lucid, elegant and dignified. It is the only remaining regular scripts by Li Yong. It is truly a treasure of inscription and is renowned as the masterpiece of stone inscription. Similar to prose in the early Tang dynasty, this article follows parallel prose style sentence pattern of the Han, Wei and Six Dynasties, with a cut-clear rhythm and full of melody. Unfortunately, due to its long age, some words are too indistinct to read. In the Song Dynasty, a horseshoe-shaped mark was left on the stone, so people also called it the Horseshoe Stele. *The Stories of Duanzhou Stone Chamber* has three unique characteristics: unique content, unique calligraphy, and unique engraving. Its value lies more in its exquisite calligraphy art.

Next, we'll explore Dragon Stone Cave, one of Seven Star Crags' key attractions. As one of the most mysterious and enjoyable caves in Seven Star Crags, Dragon Stone Cave is an important part of the cave clusters. Dragon Sone Cave, together with Green Cloud Cave and Lotus Flower Cave, makes a spectacular scene in Seven Star Crags. The cave is formulated by natural stalactite in different shapes. Some look like waterfalls and fountains, and some resemble towers and pavilions in the fairy world. It feels like standing in a magical underground palace.

Illuminated by colorful lightings, stalactites, stalagmites and dripstone curtains are well-structured in a variety of shapes. Some are like falling waterfalls, others look like towering jade pillars, and countless flower-like and coral-like stones scattered inside the caves, creating an amazing scene.

These stalactites were crystallized by the erosion of the limestone deposited through slowly dripping water during thousands of years. Hanging from cavern ceiling or rising from the floor, they appear in various shapes and form spectacular scenery. In this cave, you can enjoy the vivid stalactites such as "A Bumper Grain Harvest", "Oath of the Peach Garden", "The Lion Looking at the Camel", "The Lion Roars" and many others. Each of them embodies the uncanny masterpiece of nature.

Dear friends, please slow down your pace, and take your time to feel the gift of nature and the weight of history and the charm of culture! Thank you for listening.

四、综合知识

☆星湖旅游景区分为七星岩和鼎湖山两个片区，总面积约20平方千米。其中七星岩片区有七星岩、星湖国家湿地公园、星湖绿道，鼎湖山片区有鼎湖山。1982年经国务院批准为首批国家重点风景名胜区，2020年被评为国家5A级旅游景区、中国生态旅游示范区。

☆七星岩因七座石灰岩峰排列状如天上北斗七星而得名。有七座山峰，分别为阆风岩、玉屏岩、石室岩、天柱岩、蟾蜍岩、仙掌岩和阿坡岩；有五个湖泊，分别为仙女湖、青莲湖、中心湖、波海湖和里湖。属喀斯特岩溶地貌，有峰林、溶洞、湖泊、碑刻、道观等主要景观，被誉为"人间仙境""岭南第一奇观"。

☆七星岩石山由石灰石组成，石灰石由碳酸钙构成，容易被雨水、流水溶蚀，加上肇庆地处亚热带，雨量多，气温高，侵蚀就更为严重。随着时间推移，石山不断裸露，发育成为各种地貌形态，进一步分割成峰林石山，于是就构成了今日七星岩独特的峰林地貌。

☆在七星岩景区内可观赏到三大天象奇观：春分、秋分"卧佛含丹"，夏至"立竿无影"，冬至"月亮垂照"。

☆阆风岩是七星岩的七座岩峰之一，是七星岩的最东峰，与西峰玉屏岩对峙。"阆"意为"高大的门"，山岩像一扇巨大的铁门横亘在游人跟前。

☆玉屏岩东面与阆风岩对峙，中带横岭，状若列屏。山上有始建于明万历年间的三仙观。在三仙观后的登山道中，有两个溶洞，一大一小，一深一浅，被称为"仙人脚印"，传说是铁拐李为了保护玉屏岩顶的宝鼎，在和吕洞宾、何仙姑等一同制服偷鼎大盗时所留下的。

☆玉屏岩登山道上还有一块大石，如盾状，半截探出崖外。用石块敲击不同部位，会发出不同的声音，所以人称"八音石"，又名"扶啸台"。

☆七星岩石室岩内外留下了历代文人墨客的诗词歌赋、题字、碑名等共计500多题，是我国南方保存数量最多、最集中、质量最高的一处摩崖石刻群。其中，清代冯敏昌诗刻《七星岩五首》、黎简四言韵语《南服陨石》两石刻与唐代李邕的《端州石室记》被清代书画家黄培芳誉为"石室三绝"。经过百代积累，七星岩摩崖石刻记录下了肇庆的地理环境、山河变迁、历史大事、宗教信仰、庙宇建筑、岩石水土以及朝代变更。2001年，七星岩摩崖石刻被国务院公布为全国重点文物保护单位。

☆石刻中年代最久远的是唐代书法家、文学家李邕的《端州石室记》，是李邕唯一传世的正楷石刻。《端州石室记》有三绝：文绝、字绝、雕刻绝。由于石刻中央偏左有一马蹄形印记，所以又称马蹄碑。《端州石室记》原文386字，现存298字，描绘了七星岩石洞宛如人间仙境般的景象，并抒发了作者积极的个人抱负。

☆唐代诗人李绅（《悯农》作者）、宋代名臣包拯、诗人周敦颐（《爱莲说》作者），明代抗倭名将俞大猷，清代学者、"岭南三大家"之一屈大均等，均留下诗文题记石刻，其中更包括了罕见的南明石刻。20世纪50年代后，中华人民共和国十大元帅中的朱德、叶剑英、陈毅都曾到七星岩题诗留名，郭沫若、沈钧儒等近现代名人的诗词歌赋或题名也陆续被镌刻在崖壁上。自唐而来的各朝代石刻荟萃一堂，陈毅誉之为"千年诗廊"。

☆龙岩洞，又名石室洞，是七星岩开辟最早、景物最多的溶洞，洞内钟乳石、石笋形态各异，地形千变万化，洞口诗书成廊。双源洞是七星岩内最长的静水地下洞，洞内冬暖夏凉。

☆石室洞南口左侧，有一座依山傍水的宫殿式建筑，名为水月宫，有七星岩著名景观"水月岩云"。宫名"水月"据说是取自佛语的"镜花水月"。因景色妙趣，风光秀丽，水月宫被定为七星岩旅游风景区的标志，也是中国历史文化名城、中国优秀旅游城市肇庆的标志。

☆含珠径位于七星岩玉屏岩山腰，小径狭窄，仅通一人，峡顶嵌有一巨石，欲坠不坠，故名含珠径。叶挺曾在含珠径指挥部队反复演练，摸索出有效的攻防战术，为日后的北伐积累宝贵的实战经验。

☆仙女湖景区东北侧的狮岗炮台始建于1920年，是两广军阀混战时驻守肇庆的肇罗阳镇守使林虎为巩固城防而修建的7座炮台之一。2019年，狮岗炮台旧址被公布为广东省文物保护单位。2020年，叶挺独立团练兵场遗址（狮岗）被认定为广东省红色革命遗址。

☆"鼎湖上素"是鼎湖山庆云寺的招牌斋菜，由明代庆云寺内一位老和尚首创，传说被慈禧太后列为满汉全席名菜之一。如今鼎湖上素选取上好的冬菇、草菇、蘑菇和雪耳、木耳、榆耳、云耳、砂耳、桂花耳，配上发菜、笋干、虾米、腐竹、粉丝、黄花菜等，再加上鼎湖山的泉水烹制而成，其特点是色泽鲜艳，芳香扑鼻，吃起来甘香脆口、爽滑鲜甜。

☆"孙中山游泳处"石刻位于鼎湖山飞水潭石壁，由宋庆龄于1980年题刻。1923年7月下旬，孙中山偕夫人宋庆龄等一行来到鼎湖山游览，一边赏鼎湖山大好风景，一边商讨建国方略和北伐大计。

☆鼎湖山是我国首个自然保护区，生物多样性丰富。截至2024年1月，鼎湖山共发现新物种202种，其中以"鼎湖"或"鼎湖山"命名的物种就有44种之多。其中菌物占据了71种，如鼎湖水乳菇；动物有68种，如鼎湖黑丽金龟、鼎湖散白蚁、鼎湖头蜓；植物有63种，如鼎湖血桐、鼎湖铁线莲、鼎湖巴豆、鼎湖杜鹃。

☆鼎湖山被誉为华南生物物种的"基因储存库"和"活的自然博物馆"，原始森林里有2000多种植物，其中野生的高等植物就有1843种，占广东省植物种类的1/4，当中有被称为活化石的孑遗植物桫椤、银杏、苏铁。

肇庆市七星岩风景区

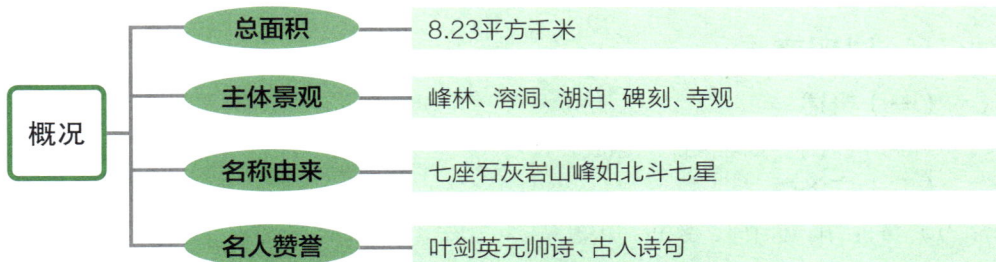

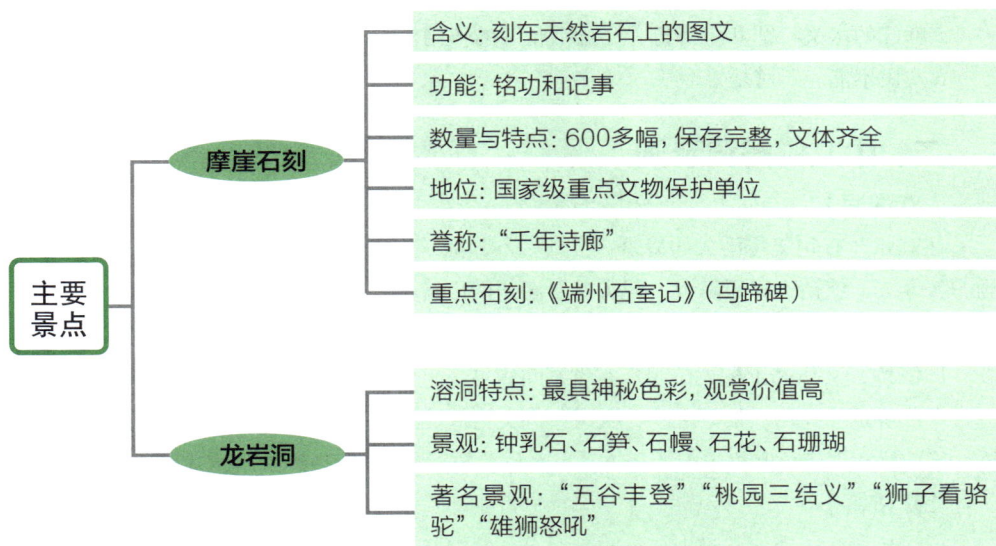

概况
- **总面积** —— 8.23平方千米
- **主体景观** —— 峰林、溶洞、湖泊、碑刻、寺观
- **名称由来** —— 七座石灰岩山峰如北斗七星
- **名人赞誉** —— 叶剑英元帅诗、古人诗句

主要景点

摩崖石刻
- 含义：刻在天然岩石上的图文
- 功能：铭功和记事
- 数量与特点：600多幅，保存完整，文体齐全
- 地位：国家级重点文物保护单位
- 誉称："千年诗廊"
- 重点石刻：《端州石室记》（马蹄碑）

龙岩洞
- 溶洞特点：最具神秘色彩，观赏价值高
- 景观：钟乳石、石笋、石幔、石花、石珊瑚
- 著名景观："五谷丰登""桃园三结义""狮子看骆驼""雄狮怒吼"

第十二节　潮州市广济桥文物旅游景区

一、讲解要点

（一）概述

广济桥的别称、地理位置、地位。

（二）广济桥

1.广济桥的修建时间、缘由、历史。

2.广济桥的长度、组成，在中国桥梁史上的地位。

3.广济桥的桥亭、石梁、桥墩。

4.西桥桥墩上的鉎牛。

5.韩江的水文特征和广济桥"浮梁结合"的作用。

6."民不能忘"牌坊。

二、中文讲解词示例

【欢迎词】

在潮州，有句流传已久的谚语："到广不到潮，枉费走一遭；到潮不到桥，白白走一场。"今天，就请大家跟随我一起去看看潮州的广济桥。

【概述】

广济桥，又称湘子桥，位于广东省潮州古城广济门外，横跨韩江，为古代闽粤交通要道。广济桥是"潮州八景"之一，全国重点文物保护单位，国家4A级旅游景区，它与赵州桥、洛阳桥和卢沟桥并称中国四大古桥。在世界桥梁史上有着独特的地位和重大的影响。

【广济桥】

广济桥始建于南宋乾道七年，也就是公元1171年。潮州太守曾汪为解决韩江两岸百姓渡江困难，造舟为梁，以86条船架设浮桥，并在河中砌一个大石墩以固定浮桥，取名"康济桥"，这是广济桥历史上第一个名字。明宣德十年，即1435年，在潮州知府王源的主持下，潮州人对桥进行了大规模的重修，改名叫"广济桥"，取"广济百粤之民"之意。明嘉靖九年，即1530年，形成"十八梭船廿四洲"的格局。目前的广济桥是2003年进行全面维修并于2007年重新启用的。

广济桥全长517.95米，由梁桥、拱桥和浮桥组成。东梁桥长283.35米，有桥墩12个、桥台1座、桥孔12个。其中东桥的第一个桥孔，采用了拱桥的造桥技术；西梁桥长137.3米，有桥墩8个、桥孔7个。连接东西梁桥的是由18条木船组成的浮桥，浮桥长97.3米。广济桥这种集梁桥、拱桥和浮桥为一体的造桥方式在我国桥梁史上还是个孤例，被桥梁专家

茅以升誉为 <u>"世界上最早的启闭式桥梁"</u> 。

广济桥的梁桥由 桥亭、石梁和桥墩 三部分组成。

桥亭 的功能是为桥身和过往行人遮风挡雨，同时能增加桥身重量，提高桥身的抗风御潮能力，延长桥的寿命。

广济桥的 桥梁 在建成后100多年时间里都是木质结构的，到了元泰定三年，即1326年，才改为石梁。广济桥的石梁硕大无比，最大的长18米，重达50吨。当年的建造者是如何将这些巨大的石梁铺架到桥墩上的呢？民间最盛行的说法是浮梁架桥法：先将船绑在大石梁上，涨潮时，利用水的浮力将船托起，将石梁固定在桥墩之间后，松绑并把船移走，石梁就架好了。

大家有没有发现？广济桥的 桥墩 是 大小不一 的。这是因为，桥墩损坏和修复年代不同，也没有按照原来的规格修复，所以桥墩的大小和形态都不同了。广济桥的 桥墩有船型墩和半船型墩两种形状。 这种六边形，上下游都做成尖形，像船的叫船型墩。那些五边形的，上游尖下游平的叫半船型墩。 尖形的桥墩可以有效地降低上游水流对大桥的冲击。 但为何将部分桥墩下游面也筑成尖形呢？据资料记载，明代以前 潮州城区曾长期受到潮水的影响， 所以将下游桥墩的形状设计为尖形。明代以后，潮水对潮州城区的影响逐渐减轻，所以部分桥墩重修时将下游一端改为方形。

【 鉎牛 】

在西桥第八个桥墩上有一只铁铸的鉎牛。雍正二年，即1724年，知府张自谦主持重修广济桥，并铸造鉎牛两只，分别放在西桥第八墩和东桥第十二墩，用来镇桥御水。后来遇到洪水，东墩的铁牛被冲倒，坠入江中，剩下现在这一只。

【 浮梁结合 】

走在广济桥的浮桥上，我们不免好奇，广济桥为何采用这种浮梁结合的结构呢？那是因为， 韩江的水流量大，如果桥墩过于密集，它的排洪能力会受到严重影响。采用这种浮梁结合的结构可以减少中间部分的桥墩，极大地减少对水流的阻力，遇到洪水，打开浮桥就能迅速排洪， 使大桥的安全性得到很大提高。另外， 白天把浮桥连接上，便于两岸老百姓渡江。晚上把浮桥拆开，可让南来北往的船只畅通无阻。 潮州广济桥每天都在为人们上演现实版的 "过河拆桥" ，这样开开合合，不知不觉度过了800多个春秋。

【 "民不能忘"牌坊 】

过完浮桥，出现在眼前的这座 "民不能忘" 牌坊，是广济桥上唯一的一座石牌坊，属德政坊，清道光年间因韩江水涨，广济桥有9个桥墩受到不同程度的破坏， 潮州知府刘浔 和分司吴均，发动民众有钱出钱有力出力。由于工程浩大，刘浔任期到了，桥还没修好，继任知府的吴均继续接力，又过了几年，终于把桥修好。老百姓感念前后两任知府的德政，集资在东桥建了"民不能忘"的牌坊以纪念他们。*提示 牌坊下的介绍文字说是潮州太守，事实上清朝没有太守这一官职。导游讲解要尊重民间俗称，更要传播正确历史知识。

【结束语】

广济桥已成为历代潮州人智慧和毅力的象征，成为所有潮州人精神家园的一个载体，承载着海内外潮人对乡情与故土的记忆。

我今天的讲解到此结束，谢谢大家！

三、英文讲解词示例

Guangji Bridge of Chaozhou

In Chaozhou, there's an old idiom: "A trip to Guangdong without visiting Chaozhou is not a complete journey; to see Chaozhou and skip the Bridge is not an enthralled journey." Today, please allow me to explore this famous Guangji Bridge with you.

Guangji Bridge, also known as Xiangzi Bridge, is located outside the ancient city gate of Chaozhou, Guangdong Province. Spanning over the Han River, it served as a crucial transportation link in ancient China. It is one of the "Eight Scenic Spots of Chaozhou", one of Major Historical and Cultural Sites Protected at the National Level, and National 4A Scenic Area. The bridge is renowned as one of China's four famous ancient bridges, the other three being Zhaozhou Bridge, Lugou Bridge, and Luoyang Bridge, holding a unique and significant place in the history of world bridge construction.

Guangji Bridge was first built by Zeng Wang, the governor of Chaozhou in the Southern Song Dynasty in 1171, who initiated the building of the bridge to solve the problem of crossing the Han River for the local people. He used 86 boats to create a pontoon bridge. It was called Kangji Bridge at that time. In 1435, during the Ming Dynasty, the bridge was extensively renovated overseen by Governor Wang Yuan, and renamed as "Guangji Bridge", meaning "The bridge benefits all people in Guangdong." The Bridge we see today underwent a comprehensive restoration in 2003 and was reopened in 2007.

Guangji Bridge is 517.95 meters long, integrating the beam bridge, arch bridge, and pontoon bridge. The eastern beam bridge stretches 283.35 meters, with 12 piers, 1 abutment, and 12 arches. The western beam bridge is 137.3 meters long, with 8 piers and 7 arches. What connects the eastern and western beam bridge is a pontoon bridge made of 18 wooden boats, spanning 97.3 meters. This unique combination of the beam, arch, and pontoon bridge elements is an isolated case of ancient bridges in China. Mao Yisheng, a Chinese bridge expert, praised it as "The World's First Open-close Bridge".

Its beam bridge section consists of pavilions, stone beams, and piers.

Pavilions serve to shield the bridge and pedestrians from wind and rain, meanwhile adding weight to the structure, enhancing its resistance to wind and waves, and extending the bridge's lifespan.

The bridge's beams were made of wood or more than 100 years after its construction. Until 1326 in Yuan Dynasty that they were replaced with stone beams. These stone beams are immense—the largest one measuring 18 meters in length and weighing around 50 tons. You probably wonder how such massive beams were placed onto the piers. According to a popular legend, here is how it's of been done: First, tie the boats to stone beams; second, wait for a high tide, which can use buoyancy of water to lift boats; third, place and fix the beams into position between the piers; lastly, untie and remove boats, and leave the beams in place.

You may notice that the piers of Guangji Bridge vary in size. This is because they were damaged and repaired at different times, with some not being restored to their original specifications, resulting in varying heights and shapes. The bridge has two types of piers: boat-shaped and semi-boat-shaped. The hexagonal piers, pointed at both sides like a boat, are called boat-shaped piers. The five-sided piers, with a sharp upstream side and a flat downstream side, are called semi-boat-shaped piers. The pointed shape effectively reduces the impact of upstream water to the bridge. But why are some piers pointed on the downstream side as well? Historical records show that Chaozhou was long affected by tidal forces before Ming Dynasty, so some downstream piers were built with pointed shapes. As the tides diminished over time, later reconstructions featured flat downstream faces.

On the eighth pier of the west bridge, you'll find an iron ox. In 1724, during the Qing dynasty, Governor Zhang Ziqian repaired the Guangji Bridge and cast two iron oxen, placing them separately at the east and west bridges. They were meant to protect the bridge. However, the eastern one was washed away by the flood. Here is the not-missing one.

As we walk across the pontoon bridge, you might wonder why Guangji Bridge was built in this way. The strong currents of the Han River are the reason. Dense piers would hinder flood discharge, so in this way, the bridge can be opened during floods to quickly release water. Plus, by day, the bridge is connected for people's easy crossing; at night, it's disconnected to allow ships to pass. You can see the view of "removing bridge to cross river" every day, which is a routine that has continued for over 800 years.

After crossing the pontoon bridge, you'll see the memorial archway carved with "Min Bu Neng Wang" meaning "people must not forget", the only stone archway on Guangji Bridge. During the Qing Dynasty, a flood severely damaged nine piers. Governors of Chaozhou, Liu Xun, and Wu Jun, mobilized the public for the repairs. The project was so extensive that it took the efforts of two governors to complete the bridge restoration. Grateful for the benevolent governance of these two, the local people pooled resources to build this "The People Must Not Forget" memorial archway on the east bridge in their honor.

Guangji Bridge has become a symbol of the wisdom and perseverance of Chaozhou people throughout the ages, serving as a spiritual anchor for all Chaozhou natives. It carries affections and memories of their homeland, cherished by Chaozhou communities both at home and abroad. This is the end of today's tour. Thank you all for your time!

四、综合知识

☆广济桥，又称湘子桥，位于潮州古城东门外，横跨韩江，联结东西两岸，为古代闽粤交通要道。是"潮州八景"之一，全国重点文物保护单位，国家4A级旅游景区，与赵州桥、洛阳桥和卢沟桥并称中国四大古桥。在潮州，有"到广不到潮，枉费走一遭；到潮不到桥，白白走一场"的民谚。

☆韩江流经潮州的河段，河面开阔，江心水急。南宋乾道七年（1171年），潮州太守曾汪为了解决百姓渡江之难，以86艘船相互连接而成浮桥，并把这座浮桥命名为"康济桥"。

☆明嘉靖九年（1530年），知府丘其仁将江心的24梭船减至18只梭船，至此广济桥形成了"十八梭船廿四洲"的独特格局。"洲"指的是广济桥的桥墩，因为体积庞大像四面环水的陆地，因此称之为"洲"。

☆南宋淳熙元年（1174年），知州常祎重修广济桥，浮舟增至106艘，并开启了在桥上修建亭屋的先河。广济桥上每座楼阁的建筑风格和两面楹联匾额都各不相同，从东西两岸看都是不同的"十二样"，于是被民众称赞为"廿四楼台廿四样"。广济桥上形式各异的亭台楼阁是该桥的一大奇观，因兼作经商店铺，故有"一里长桥一里市"之美称。

☆清雍正二年（1724年），知府张自谦修缮广济桥，铸鉎牛二只以镇桥御水。铸牛资金不够，张自谦便倡议当地士绅捐款，各方纷纷响应。据传，负责铸牛工程的是曾经慷慨解囊、帮助张自谦的炉商邓荣登。得知邓荣登家道中落、经济困难，张自谦便将铸牛工程交给邓荣登，使邓荣登缴清了积欠的炉饷。

☆其中一只鉎牛被洪水冲走后，仅剩西岸一只鉎牛。民间有"潮州湘桥好风流，十八梭船廿四洲。廿四楼台廿四样，二只鉎牛一只溜"的歌谣。1958年，在广济桥改建清基过程中，人们发现那只丢失的鉎牛被沉压在桥墩之下，便把它打捞上来。20世纪80年代初，依原样重铸两只鉎牛，为贴合"二只鉎牛一只溜"的历史，仅一只鉎牛立于广济桥西洲，另一只鉎牛则立于潮州城东的砚峰。

☆2003年3月，广济桥修复工程动工，按明代风格修复，桥中部恢复为浮桥，桥墩上建亭台楼阁。2007年9月竣工，再现了广济桥梁舟结合、重瓴联阁的风姿，并作为旅游观光步行桥对游客开放。

☆明代，韩江流域的商业逐渐兴起，潮州因其地理位置成为韩江流域经济中心，航行于韩江的盐商经过广济桥赴各地销售。明代中后期，潮州的海外贸易开始发达，货物通过广济桥往来南北。到清代，潮州城已成为仅次于广州的广东省第二大商业中心。

☆广济桥集梁桥、浮桥、拱桥于一体，风格独特。桥梁专家茅以升曾撰文指出，广济桥中有一段，用船只连为浮桥，可以解开，让出航道，成为可分可合的活动桥，是我国桥梁史上的一个特例，是"世界上最早的启闭式桥梁"。

☆"民不能忘"牌坊，是广济桥上唯一的一座石牌坊。清代，潮州老百姓为纪念刘浔、吴均两位知府重修广济桥的功绩，集资修建。

☆广济桥的桥墩有两种墩型，船型墩和半船型墩。桥墩较大，可以应对强大径流，但如修得又大又密，将使桥梁的排洪能力受到严重影响。浮梁结合的结构可以减少中间部分的桥墩，极大地减少对径流的阻力，打开浮桥还能迅速排洪，既提高了大桥的排洪能力，又提高了大桥的安全性。

潮州市广济桥文物旅游景区

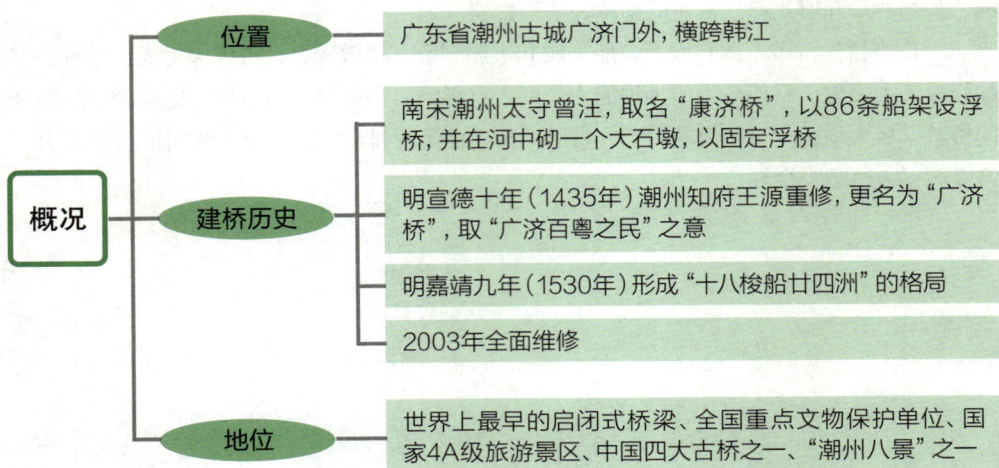

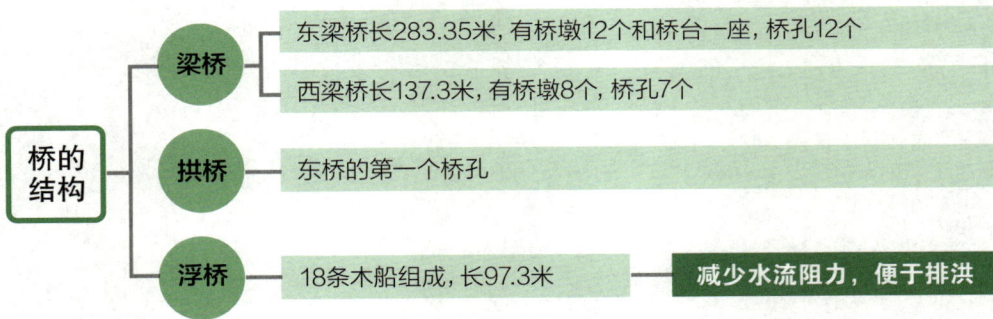

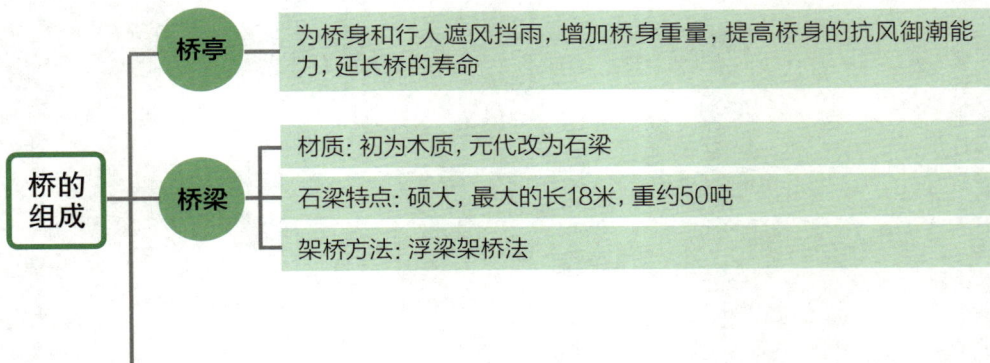

位置 —— 广东省潮州古城广济门外,横跨韩江

概况

建桥历史
- 南宋潮州太守曾汪,取名"康济桥",以86条船架设浮桥,并在河中砌一个大石墩,以固定浮桥
- 明宣德十年(1435年)潮州知府王源重修,更名为"广济桥",取"广济百粤之民"之意
- 明嘉靖九年(1530年)形成"十八梭船廿四洲"的格局
- 2003年全面维修

地位 —— 世界上最早的启闭式桥梁、全国重点文物保护单位、国家4A级旅游景区、中国四大古桥之一、"潮州八景"之一

桥的结构

梁桥
- 东梁桥长283.35米,有桥墩12个和桥台一座,桥孔12个
- 西梁桥长137.3米,有桥墩8个,桥孔7个

拱桥 —— 东桥的第一个桥孔

浮桥 —— 18条木船组成,长97.3米 —— **减少水流阻力,便于排洪**

桥的组成

桥亭 —— 为桥身和行人遮风挡雨,增加桥身重量,提高桥身的抗风御潮能力,延长桥的寿命

桥梁
- 材质:初为木质,元代改为石梁
- 石梁特点:硕大,最大的长18米,重约50吨
- 架桥方法:浮梁架桥法

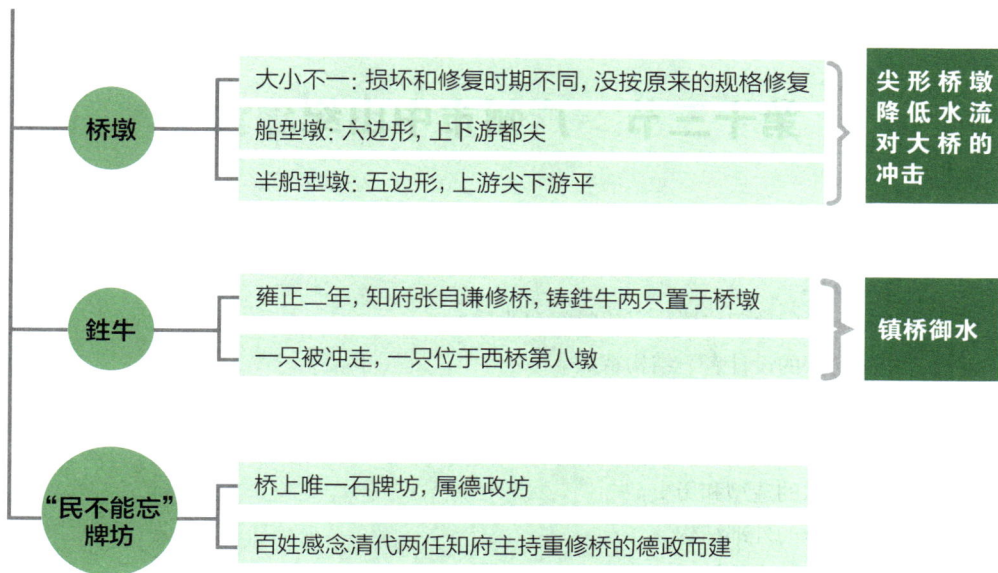

桥墩
- 大小不一: 损坏和修复时期不同, 没按原来的规格修复
- 船型墩: 六边形, 上下游都尖
- 半船型墩: 五边形, 上游尖下游平

尖形桥墩降低水流对大桥的冲击

鉎牛
- 雍正二年, 知府张自谦修桥, 铸鉎牛两只置于桥墩
- 一只被冲走, 一只位于西桥第八墩

镇桥御水

"民不能忘"牌坊
- 桥上唯一石牌坊, 属德政坊
- 百姓感念清代两任知府主持重修桥的德政而建

第十三节　广州市中山纪念堂

一、讲解要点

（一）概述

1.中山纪念堂的地理位置、兴建时间和背景。

2.中山纪念堂的设计者、结构特点。

3.中山纪念堂的价值和地位。

（二）中山纪念堂

1.孙中山铜像的造型和历史。

2.中山纪念堂的外部结构。

3.中山纪念堂的内部结构。

4.总理遗嘱碑刻的造型。

5."木棉王"的树龄和荣誉。

二、中文讲解词示例

【欢迎词】

伟人事迹人人称颂，中山精神世代流传。各位游客，大家好！欢迎来到广州中山纪念堂。

【概述】

广州中山纪念堂坐落在越秀山南麓，是广州近代城市中轴线上的重要节点、广州标志性建筑。1921年5月至1922年6月期间，孙中山先生曾在此就任中华民国非常大总统。1925年孙中山先生逝世后，广州人民为了纪念这位伟大的革命先行者，在总统府的旧址上建造了中山纪念堂。广州中山纪念堂于1928年动工，1929年奠基，1931年落成，总占地面积6.1万平方米，包括大堂四周平台的主体建筑总占地面积共1.2万平方米，堂高49米，是当时亚洲最大的会堂式建筑和目前全球最大的孙中山纪念堂。

广州中山纪念堂由近代著名的建筑师吕彦直先生设计，以中西合璧的建筑形式，成为世界建筑宝库中的瑰宝。如今，广州中山纪念堂集纪念、旅游、集会和演出为一体，是全国重点文物保护单位、国家4A级旅游景区，也是广州的历史名片。

【孙中山铜像】

大家看，现在呈现在我们面前的就是伟人孙中山的铜像。这座铜像高5.5米，重达3.9吨。铜像下白色花岗岩的基座上，镌刻着孙中山先生所著的《建国大纲》内容。

大家知道吗？孙中山铜像与下面的基座其实并非同时落成的。广州中山纪念堂建成后，由于条件所限，一时无法建造铜像，只在主体建筑前预留了铜像基座。1954年，中山大学内的孙中山铜像被借来在此摆放，但是由于中山大学的孙中山铜像体量太小，与纪念堂建筑物和广场的整体规模不相称，因此广州市人民委员会决定铸造新像。1958年，著名雕塑家尹积昌先生设计并制作了一座以水泥为基体、外层镀上铜粉的仿铜质感孙中山像。从此，广州中山纪念堂有了自己的第一座孙中山像。

1998年广州中山纪念堂大修以后，按尹积昌作品原样塑造的新孙中山铜像登上了基座，铜像生动再现了孙中山先生在岭南大学演讲时的造型，这就是我们今天看到的孙中山铜像的样子。*提示 讲述建筑故事，引起游客情感共鸣。

【外部结构】

广州中山纪念堂是一座宏伟、壮丽的八角形宫殿式建筑。整座建筑面积约为3700平方米，高49米，由前后左右四个宫殿式重檐歇山抱厦建筑组成。堂顶是宝蓝色的琉璃瓦，攒尖式汇聚于宝顶之上。宝顶呈椭圆形，由三万多块法国金箔玻璃马赛克镶砌，在阳光的照耀下显得光彩夺目。红柱黄墙衬着蓝色的琉璃瓦，再加上金光灿灿的宝顶，使整体建筑显得既庄严典雅又气势恢宏。*提示 可对装饰细节进行描述和视觉化呈现。

大堂正面悬挂着孙中山手写的金字牌匾——"天下为公"，寓意国、为人民所共有，政治为人民所共管，利益为人民所共享，是孙中山先生民主思想的体现。

【内部结构】

广州中山纪念堂的建筑结构非常巧妙，大堂空间开阔，装饰风格浓郁，充满中式传统特色。为了满足纪念堂起初作为大型集会场所的要求，吕彦直大胆地采用的西方钢结构和钢筋混凝土建筑技术，突破了中国传统木结构对大空间的限制，创造性地使用中国古建筑手法，将一系列建筑构件精巧地结合在一起。

大堂南北宽71米。观众席分楼上楼下两层，有8座楼梯，11个进出口，共有3000个座位。那么各位可能很惊讶，这么大的大堂，怎么会看不到一根柱子支撑顶盖呢？原来这里共有8根柱子，但都藏在周围的内墙里，支撑着顶盖的8个角。由于柱子都藏在墙里，观众无论坐在哪个位置，观看舞台的视线都不会受阻。而且堂内没有回音，即使你坐在最远的角落，都能清晰地听到舞台的音响。这些都是纪念堂设计的巧妙之处。

【总理遗嘱碑刻】

大家请往舞台上看，舞台的后墙中央有一块汉白玉石碑，上面刻有孙中山先生浮雕头像和《总理遗嘱》，四周环绕缠枝莲纹和祥云边框。石碑高2.41米、宽1.9米，显得气势非凡，庄严肃穆。

【"木棉王"】

纪念堂旁还有一株被称为"木棉王"的木棉树。这株栽植于1669年前后的古树，如今已有350余岁高龄，在2018年全国范围内组织开展的"中国最美古树"遴选活动中，"木棉王"荣获了"中国最美木棉"称号。

【结束语】

走在这座辉煌的建筑里，细细品味这里的一砖一瓦，我们会欣赏到博大精深的中国建筑艺术，惊叹设计师丰富的想象力和非凡的设计才能，感悟到孙中山天下为公的伟人情怀。我的讲解到此结束，谢谢大家！

三、英文讲解词示例

Sun Yat-sen's Memorial Hall in Guangzhou

Sun Yat-sen's contributions are praised by the world, and Sun Yat-sen's spirit is inherited over generations. Hello! everyone, welcome to Sun Yat-sen's Memorial Hall in Guangzhou.

Located at the southern foot of Yuexiu Hill, the Memorial Hall is an important node on the central axis and a landmark of modern Guangzhou. From May 1921 to June 1922, Dr. Sun Yat-sen served as the Special President of the Republic of China. Therefore, residents of Guangzhou built Sun Yat-sen's Memorial Hall on the former site of the Presidential Palace in order to commemorate this great revolutionary pioneer after his death in 1925. The construction of the Memorial Hall was started in 1928, and the foundation was laid in 1929. In 1931, the construction was finally completed. The Memorial Hall covers a total area of 61,000 square meters. The main building covers an area of 12,000 square meters, including the platforms around the auditorium. The hall is 48.63 meters high. It was the largest hall in Asia at that time and it is the largest existing Sun Yat-sen Memorial Hall in the world.

Designed by Mr. Lyu Yanzhi, a famous architect in modern China, Sun Yat-sen's Memorial Hall is renowned as the treasure of the world with its great combination of Chinese and Western styles. Today, the Memorial Hall integrates functions of memorial, tourism, assembly and performance. It is a Major Historical and Cultural Site Protected at the National Level, a National 4A Scenic Area, and a historical name-card of Guangzhou.

Please take a look ahead. It is the bronze statue of the great man—Dr. Sun Yat-sen. It is 5.5 meters high and weighs 3.9 tons. The white granite base under the bronze statue is engraved with the content of *The Outline of the Founding of the National Government* written by Dr. Sun.

Actually, the statue and the granite base were not built at the same time. When the Memorial Hall was competed, the bronze statue could not be built on time due to the limited conditions. Therefore, only the base was set in front of the main building. In 1954, a bronze statue was borrowed from Sun Yat-sen University and placed here, but its size was too small and did not match the entire layout of the Memorial Hall and the square. Thus, a new statue was needed. Four years later, in 1958, Mr. Yin Jichang, a famous sculptor, designed and produced a statue of Dr. Sun Yat-sen with cement as the base material and copper powder on the outer layer. It was the first statue that belonged to the Memorial Hall itself.

In 1998, after a major repair of Sun Yat-sen Memorial Hall, a new bronze statue of Sun

Yat-sen, modeled after Yin's work, replaced the first one. The bronze statue vividly reproduces the shape of Dr. Sun Yat-sen's speech at Lingnan University. It is what we see today.

The Memorial Hall is a grand, magnificent octagonal palace building. Its floor space is about 3,700 square meters, and it is 49 meters high. On its four sides, there are 4 buildings with double-eave gable and hip roofs. It is a typically traditional palace style architecture in ancient China. The round pavilion roofs of the hall are capped with royal blue glazed tiles to form a roof crown. The roof crown is elliptical in shape and is set with more than 30,000 French gold glass mosaics, shining brightly in the sun. Red pillars, yellow walls, royal blue glazed tiles and the golden roof crown, make the whole building exquisite, elegant and imposing.

On the front of the hall hangs a plaque with four golden characters "Tian Xia Wei Gong" written by Dr. Sun Yat-sen. This slogan means that the country, the government, and the national interests are shared by the people. It is the embodiment of his democratic thought.

The architectural structure of the Memorial Hall is indeed ingenious. It has a spacious auditorium and a fascinating traditional Chinese style decoration. To meet the needs of large scale gathering or assembly, Lyu boldly adopted Western steel structure and reinforced concrete construction techniques, a great breakthrough from the traditional Chinese wooden structure. He creatively applied ancient Chinese architectural techniques and skillfully combined a series of building components.

The auditorium is 71 meters wide on the four sides. It is divided into two floors, with eight staircases, 11 entrances and exits, and a total of 3,000 seats. Look around, and you may wonder there is no pillar supporting the rooftop, in such a large auditorium. In fact, there are 8 pillars, but they are all hidden in the surrounding walls. Therefore, the audience's view of the stage is not influenced or blocked. Do you notice that there is no echo in the hall? Even if you sit in the farthest corner, you can clearly hear the sound from the stage. Smart design, right?

Everyone, please look at the stage. In the center of the background wall of the stage, there is a white marble tablet. It is engraved with the head relief sculpture of Dr. Sun Yat-sen and next to it is _the Premier's Last Will and Testament_. It is framed with laced lotuses and auspicious clouds. The tablet measures 2.41 meters high and 1.9 meters wide. It is remarkable and solemn.

In the Memorial Hall, there is a kapok tree called "The King of Kapok Trees". Planted in 1669 or so, it is now more than 350 year old. In 2018, it was awarded as "The Most Beautiful Kapok Tree" in activity of selecting the most beautiful ancient trees in China.

Walking through the hall, immersing ourselves here with the bricks and tiles, you may have read few pages of the history and the art of Chinese architectures. Hope you enjoy the journey, amazed by the intelligence and smart designs of the buildings, the history and great wills of Dr. Sun Yat-sen as a pioneer of the revolution. It is the end of our tour. Thank you so much for your time.

四、综合知识

☆广州中山纪念堂在整体色彩上，以蓝、白、红三色为主色调。青色彩绘、蓝色琉璃瓦象征青天；白色穹顶象征白日；红色门窗、柱子象征满地红。"青天白日满地红旗"是孙中山为中华民国选择的国旗，寓意"光明正照"和"自由、平等、博爱"，代表了孙中山的革命理想。

☆整个广州中山纪念堂建筑群采用中轴对称的传统手法，中轴线的最前方为正门楼，总平面正中央屹立着孙中山先生的全身铜像，铜像后面是中山纪念堂，而中轴线的后端则是越秀山顶上高耸的中山纪念碑。

☆广州中山纪念堂由我国著名建筑师吕彦直先生所设计。他设计的这座中山纪念堂，在外形上具有中国传统建筑艺术风格，在结构上则采用了当时最新的建筑技术，既华丽壮观，又能适应现代集会的需要，在国内堪称首创。除了中山纪念堂外，他还设计了南京中山陵和广州市越秀公园的纪念碑，同样是孙中山先生的纪念性建筑。

☆广州中山纪念堂主体建筑的东西两侧各生长着一株古白兰树，至今已有近120年树龄，属于古树名木，是广州树荫覆盖面积最大的白兰树。长青的古白兰象征孙中山先生为之奋斗的革命事业万古长青，香味醇郁的白色花朵象征着孙中山先生的革命精神流芳百世，香留人间。

☆广州中山纪念堂主体建筑前东西两侧各有一个宝蓝色的大陶鼎，东侧的是1929年6月1日为纪念孙中山的奉安大典而制作的；西侧的是1930年11月为纪念纪念堂落成而制作的。鼎身除了刻有《总理遗嘱》外，后面还有四个大字"万世昭垂"。鼎身的字体和花纹有所脱落，但整体保存完好。

☆广州中山纪念堂前大草坪的东西两侧，各有一根云鹤华表，建于1931年。按照吕彦直的原设计，华表柱头为山羊造型，象征"羊城"广州，后改建为云鹤造型，云鹤华表也因此得名。云鹤华表寓意吉祥、祝福，同时也表达了人们对孙中山先生的崇敬之情。

☆承托纪念堂的是用香港花岗岩砌造的台基，台基为须弥座造型。每个出入口均设置两段阶梯，同样是用花岗岩砌筑，一段为五级，一段为九级，暗合"九五之尊"，表达了对孙中山先生的尊崇。

☆纪念堂的舞台上有一块汉白玉石碑，上面刻有孙中山浮雕头像和总理遗嘱的内容。石碑高2.41米，宽1.9米，四周环绕缠枝莲纹和祥云边框。"曹全碑体"的总理遗嘱碑刻是吴子复的手迹，由广东端州的梁俊生镌刻。

☆广州中山纪念堂的主体建筑上，每一根圆柱的柱头饰都刻着与人民币的货币符号（¥）完全一致的符号。据纪念堂管理处工作人员推测，该符号是一个"羊"字，可能与羊城"五羊献穗"的美丽传说有关，意即"羊城的中山纪念堂"和"羊城人民对孙中山的永远怀念之情"。

　　☆广州中山纪念堂以及它所在的这片土地，是广州城市历史的见证者，承载着一段段重要的历史记忆。1935年，高考广州区试场设在广州中山纪念堂。1945年9月16日，广东侵华日军受降仪式在广州中山纪念堂举行。1950年10月1日，广州市各界庆祝中华人民共和国国庆节大会在广州中山纪念堂举行，人民群众欢聚一堂。2008年5月7日，北京奥运圣火在广州传递，途经广州中山纪念堂。

　　☆1958年1月24日，毛泽东参观广州中山纪念堂。他称许说："这是中国人自己设计、自己施工建造的伟大建筑物，谁说中国人不行？"

　　☆中山纪念堂内一共有29株木棉树，其中有一株被称为"木棉王"。2024年3月，中山纪念堂举行第三届木棉文化节，组织了近50场文化活动，全面呈现具有岭南文化特质、融合广州红棉精神的优秀文化成果。

广州市中山纪念堂

概况
- 纪念对象: 孙中山
- 设计者: 吕彦直
- 建设时间: 1925—1931年
- 地点: 孙中山总统府旧址
- 规模: 占地面积6.1万平方米, 主体建筑面积1.2万平方米
- 功能: 纪念、旅游、集会、演出
- 荣誉: 全国重点文物保护单位、国家4A级旅游景区、广州的历史名片

孙中山铜像
- 造型: 在岭南大学演讲时的形象
- 基座: 镌刻《建国大纲》

主体建筑——大礼堂
- **外观**
  - 高度: 49米
  - 结构: 钢筋混凝土, 宫殿式
  - 屋顶: 八角攒尖重檐歇山顶, 宝蓝色琉璃瓦
  - 装饰: 红柱黄砖, 彩画图案
  - 特色元素: "天下为公"大匾, 朱色水磨大石柱
- **内部**
  - 宽度: 71米
  - 特色: 8根柱子藏在墙内
  - 舞台与观众席: 上下两层观众席, 8座楼梯, 3000个座位

总理遗嘱碑刻
- 汉白玉石碑, 刻有孙中山浮雕头像和《总理遗嘱》

"木棉王"
- 350余岁高龄, "中国最美木棉"

第十四节　广州市南越王博物院（王墓展区）

一、讲解要点

（一）概述

南越王墓发现时间、背景以及在考古界的地位。

（二）南越王墓

1.墓室的结构。

2.赵佗和墓主人赵眜。

3."文帝行玺"金印的造型和出土状态。

4.丝缕玉衣的组成和用途。

5.透雕龙凤纹重环玉佩的纹样。

二、中文讲解词示例

【欢迎词】

大家好！欢迎大家来到南越王博物院参观！

【概述】

南越王博物院是以南越国重要考古遗存为依托的大型考古遗址类博物馆，分为王墓和王宫两个展区。

南越王墓是怎么被发现的呢？1980年，广东省政府计划在象岗山修建宿舍楼，1983年动工挖墙基的时候，发现了这座深埋于山中达2000多年的南越王墓，从此揭开了南越国的神秘面纱。

这座墓室是岭南地区规模最大、随葬品最丰富、墓主人等级最高的汉代彩绘石室墓，共出土了文物1000多件（套）。1996年，南越王墓被列为全国重点文物保护单位，被誉为"岭南文化之光"。2021年，南越王墓及南越国宫署遗址入选"百年百大考古发现"。

【墓室】

王墓位于象岗山，海拔49.71米。从空中俯瞰，山的形状就像一只大象，所以叫象岗山。南越国第二代王赵眜的墓就在这里凿山为藏，深埋于20多米的山腹深处，历史上从来没有被盗扰过。墓室建筑面积约100平方米，仿阳宅格局建造，中轴对称、坐北朝南、前朝后寝，共7室，分别为前室、东耳室、西耳室、主棺室、东侧室、西侧室和后藏室，每间室的功能都不相同。墓内还发现有15个殉人，体现了"事死如事生"的丧葬观念。建墓所用的750块红砂岩石料来自现在的广州番禺区莲花山，当时的采石场距离象岗山有二十海里，可见工程浩大。

大家觉得文物会说话吗？接下来让我们一起去展厅参观从南越王墓中出土的文物，看看它们能告诉我们2000多年前哪些历史故事。

【南越国历史】

这个展览名为"南越藏珍"，展示了南越王墓中出土的文物。这些墓室的随葬品让我们了解到南越王生前吃有山珍海味，穿有绫罗绸缎，行有车马仪仗，乐有宫廷宴乐。这小小的墓室就像是南越王去世后居住的地下宫殿。

您知道曾经被毛泽东高度评价为"南下干部第一人"的是谁吗？他是秦始皇派来攻打岭南的一位将领，是南越国的第一位王——赵佗。赵佗在公元前203年建立了南越国，比刘邦建立西汉还早一年。赵佗推行"和辑百越"的政策，为维护统一、改善民生、凝聚人心、实现南北各民族共同繁荣作出了巨大贡献。

南越国一共经历了五代王，跨越了93年。由于赵佗太长寿，活了103岁，他的儿子都熬不过他先他而去，赵佗就把王位传给了孙子，也就是象岗山汉墓的墓主人赵眜。公元前111年汉武帝派汉军南下火烧了南越王宫，南越国从此灭亡。

【"文帝行玺"金印】

我们现在看到的这枚金印是南越文王的官印。出土时放在墓主人胸部偏右的位置，印面阴刻有小篆体"文帝行玺"四个字，书体工整，刚健有力。金印的印钮是一条盘曲的游龙，龙头伸向一角，似乎正准备腾空跳跃，龙身上的鳞片和爪是铸成后再凿刻的，龙腰隆起形成的空隙是用来穿印绶的。

出土的时候，金印印面沟槽及印台四壁有碰痕和划伤，还看到附着暗红色的印泥；在印钮龙身隆起的部位，肉眼能看到两侧摩擦得特别光滑，有使用过的痕迹，可推测它是墓主生前的实用物。这枚"文帝行玺"金印是我国目前考古发现的最大的一枚西汉金印。

【丝缕玉衣】

现在我们一起来欣赏这件我国出土的年代较早的一套形制完备的丝缕玉衣。为什么墓主人身穿玉衣而且玉衣上下还铺满玉璧呢？因为当时的人迷信玉，认为玉衣可以使尸体不腐，引导灵魂升天。

汉制规定，有金缕、银缕和铜缕玉衣，按等级不同分级使用。这件玉衣由2291块玉片组成，丝带纵横交叉将玉片粘接在一起，背面贴衬丝绢或麻布固定而成。玉衣长1.73米，由此可推测墓主人身高1米7左右。我们从脚到头观察一下：墓主人脚底有块玉，双连玉璧，寓意踩璧升天；他的手里也握着玉，寓意死后照样掌握权力和财富；头顶居然还有个孔，可能是便于灵魂出窍。这些充分反映了南越国统治者的崇玉观念和厚葬习俗。

【透雕龙凤纹重环玉佩】

这件玉佩是透雕龙凤纹重环玉佩，发现于墓主右眼位置。它分为内外两圈，内圈的游龙像在腾飞游动，龙的前爪和尾巴都伸到外圈，在龙的前爪上站着一只体态轻盈的凤鸟，凤鸟的冠和尾羽延伸成卷云纹把外圈空间填满。美丽的凤鸟回头跟龙对望，好像在对话的样子。这件玉佩构图完美和谐，主次分明，充满动感灵气，是玉饰中的精品。这个图案被选为我们南越王博物院的院徽，同时它也是广州市城市原点标志的设计元素之一。

【结束语】

南越王博物院承载着岭南文化两千余年的历史底蕴，是中华文明多元一体格局的重要见证。我的讲解到此结束，感谢各位的聆听。

三、英文讲解词示例

Nanyue King Museum (the King's Mausoleum Exhibition Site) in Guanghzou

Hello everyone! Welcome to visit the Nanyue King Museum! I am your tour guide.

The Nanyue King Museum is a large-scale archaeological site museum based on the important remains of the Nanyue Kingdom. There are two exhibition sites: the King's Mausoleum and the Palace.

How was the mausoleum discovered? In 1980, the Guangdong provincial government planned to build a dormitory building in Mount Xianggang. In 1983, when the work started to set up the wall base setting, the workers discovered the tomb of Nanyue King, which had been buried in the mountains for more than 2,000 years. This is how the mystery of the Nanyue Kingdom was unveiled.

It is the largest color-painted stone tomb of the Han Dynasty in Lingnan region, with the richest funerary objects and the highest level of tomb owner. More than 1,000 pieces (sets) of cultural relics have been unearthed. In 1996, the Nanyue King's Tomb was listed as a Major Historical and Cultural Site Protected at the National Level, and was called "The Glory of Lingnan Culture". In 2021, both the site of Nanyue King's Mausoleum and the site of Nanyue Palace were praised as the "100 Archaeological Discoveries in the Past 100 Years".

The King's Mausoleum is located in Mount Xianggang, with an altitude of only 49.71 meters. From a bird's eye view, it is shaped like an elephant, which is pronounced "Xiang". So it is called Mount Xianggang. The Mausoleum of Zhao Mo, the second ruler of Nanyue Kingdom, is located here. The mausoleum covers an area of about 100 square meters and was built like a regular house with 7 rooms: the front room, the east room, the west room, the main coffin room, the east side room, the west side room and the back room. Each room serves different functions. 15 sacrificial victims were found in the tomb, which shows the funeral concept of serving the dead like serving the alive. The 750 red sandstones used to construct the mausoleum were transported from the current Mount Lianhua in Panyu District, Guangzhou. At that time, those stones were 20 sea miles away from Mount Xianggang. It meant that the project was very grand.

Do you believe that the cultural relics speak for themselves? Now, let's move to the exhibition hall and have a look at the cultural relics and learn some historical stories more than 2,000 years ago.

This exhibition is called *the Treasures from the Mausoleum of Nanyue King*. The burial articles will let us know that the Nanyue King lived with rare delicacies to eat, silks and satins to wear, chariots and harnesses to ride, and music and banquets to enjoy. This small tomb is like an underground palace for the Nanyue King after his death.

Do you know who was once highly praised by Chairman Mao Zedong "The First Official Going South"? He was Zhao Tuo, the first ruler of the Nanyue Kingdom. As a general, he was sent to attack Lingnan by Qin Shi Huang, the first emperor of a unified China. Zhao Tuo established Nanyue Kingdom in 203 BC, one year earlier than Liu Bang established the Western Han Dynasty. Zhao Tuo carried out the policy of harmony and integration with the surrounding groups to ensure unity and improve people's wellbeing.

The Nanyue Kingdom witnessed five kings, spanning 93 years. Because Zhao Tuo lived a very long life, and died at 103, even his sons died before him. Zhao Tuo passed on the throne to his grandson, namely Zhao Mo, the owner of Mount Xianggang Mausoleum. In 111 BC, Emperor Wu of the Han Dynasty sent troops south to burn down the Nanyue Palace, and the Nanyue Kingdom was then destroyed.

This gold seal is the "Administrative Seal of Emperor Wen", the official seal of Emperor Wen. It was on the right side of the mausoleum owner's chest when discovered. The seal surface was incised "Wen Di Xing Xi" in Xiaozhuan style of calligraphy. This gold seal is supposed to be the official seal of the Nanyue Emperor Wen. The seal knob is a coiled Chinese dragon, the head stretching as if it is jumping into the air. The dragon's scales and claws were cast and then chiseled, and the space under the Chinese dragon's waist is left for the seal ribbon.

When unearthed, there were bumps and scratches on the groove of the gold seal surface and the four walls of the stamp pad attached with dark red inkpad. At the seal knob where the Chinese dragon's body was raised, we could see that the two sides are very smooth, meaning it was worn smooth when used, so we can guess that it was a useful tool for the mausoleum owner in his life. This gold seal is the largest gold seal of the Western Han Dynasty discovered in China so far.

Now let's appreciate the earlier set of complete Jade Burial Suit Sewn with Silk Thread in China by now. Why does the owner of the mausoleum wear a jade shroud? People living in the Han Dynasty believed that jade shroud could keep the body from rotting and guide the soul to heaven.

According to the system of the Han Dynasty, there are gold thread, silver thread and copper thread jade clothes, which were used for officials at different levels. This jade shroud consists of 2,291 jade pieces. They are put together by crossing ribbons, and fixed by silk or linen on the back. The jade shroud is 1.73 meters long, so it can be inferred that the owner of the mausoleum is about 1.7 meters tall. Let's look at it from the bottom. There is a piece of jade under each foot of the owner of the mausoleum, which means stepping on the jade to ascend to heaven. He also holds jade in his hand, which means that he still holds power and wealth after death. There is actually a hole at the top of the head, which may allow the soul to come out of the body. These signs fully reflect that the Nanyue rulers' love of jade and the custom of grand burial.

This jade pendant is a double-ring openwork carving with Chinese dragon and phoenix. It was found near the mausoleum owner's right eye. It has an inner circle and an outer circle. The dragon in the inner circle seems soaring and swimming, and its front paws and tail extend beyond the inner circle. On one of the Chinese dragon's front paws, there stands a lissome phoenix. The crown and tail feathers of the phoenix extend into the rolling cloud pattern to fill the space of the outer circle. The beautiful phoenix looks back at the Chinese dragon, as if they were talking. This jade disk comes with perfect and harmonious and dynamic pattern and is a premium jade work. This pattern was chosen as the emblem of the Nanyue King Museum, and it is also one of the design components of the Guangzhou Zero Point Logo.

The Nanyue King Museum bears the history of Lingnan culture for over 2,000 years, and it is an important witness to the diverse Chinese civilization. This is the end of the tour. Thank you for listening.

四、综合知识

☆南越王博物院是以南越国重要考古遗存为依托的大型考古遗址类博物馆，为国家一级博物馆，分为王墓和王宫两个展区。

☆王宫展区以南越国宫署遗址为核心，被誉为"广州历史文化名城的精华所在"。王墓展区以1983年发现的南越文王墓为核心，被誉为"岭南文化之光"。

☆南越文王墓和南越国宫署遗址集中展现了秦汉时期岭南地区政治、经济和文化的发展状况，二者均为全国重点文物保护单位，于2021年入选"百年百大考古发现"。

☆1995年发现的"石构水池"和1997年发现的"曲流石渠"组成的南越国御苑遗址，位于南越国宫署遗址，是目前发现年代较早、保存较为完好的秦汉宫苑实例，入选当年"全国十大考古新发现"。在楼顶花园，还能看到一条模拟复原的曲流石渠，有小桥、步石与亭台楼阁。

☆曲流石渠结尾处的木暗槽，是南越国宫署排水系统的一部分。木暗槽使用的木材为杉木，生长快，耐腐力强，不受白蚁蛀食，且长期埋藏于地下，虽然潮湿，但隔绝了空气，所以保存完好。

☆南越国宫署遗址的考古地层关键柱，展示了叠压了自秦汉至民国共13个历史时期的文化层，是一部反映广州两千多年城市发展历史的无字史书。

☆南越文王墓是南越国第二代王赵眜之墓。该墓是岭南地区规模最大、随葬品最丰富、墓主人等级最高的汉代彩绘石室墓，墓中共出土1000多件（套）文物，其中"文帝行玺"金印、犀角形玉杯、丝缕玉衣等具有重要历史价值。

☆王墓展区由主体陈列楼、综合陈列楼和古墓保护区三部分组成，基本陈列分为"秦汉南疆"南越国历史专题陈列、"南越藏珍"西汉南越王墓出土文物陈列和杨永德伉俪捐赠藏枕专题陈列。

☆犀角形玉杯通体由一整块青白玉雕琢而成，杯壁呈半透明状，局部有红褐色浸斑，杯口呈椭圆状，杯腹中空可盛酒，整体看上去颇似一只犀牛角。这种角形杯又叫"来通杯"，被认为发端于爱琴文明，犀角形玉杯是广州地区西汉时期中外交流的又一见证。

☆"文帝行玺"金印是目前所见西汉最大金印，也是发现的最早以龙为钮的帝王玺印。出土时放在墓主人的胸部偏右的位置，印面阴刻有小篆体"文帝行玺"四个字。

☆以龙为帝玺钮是南越国首创。据推测，金印上的龙应当属于"猪鼻龙"，与龙山文化所见玉龙头部比较接近，可能与远古时期猪在畜牧业中的地位，以及当时龙的形象尚未定型有关。

☆南越王博物院的院徽图案取自透雕龙凤纹重环玉佩。玉佩发现于墓主右眼位置，圆璧形的内圈透雕一游龙，两爪及尾部伸向外圈，外圈透雕一凤鸟，立于龙爪之上。鸟冠及尾羽均为卷云纹，把外圈上下填满。

☆"南越王博物院"院名的字体，前五字集自南越国宫署遗址出土的南越木简，木简出土于宫署遗址内的一口南越国时期的井里；最后一个"院"字，则是从南越木简、里耶秦简与云梦秦简中，分别集出笔画进行重组，并美化字形结构而成。里耶与云梦均属楚地，南越王墓中出土了多件含有楚文化元素的精品文物。

☆丝缕玉衣由2291片玉片、丝缕和麻布粘贴编缀而成，分为头套、上身衣、袖筒、手套、裤筒和鞋六部分，全长1.73米，是我国出土的年代较早的一套形制完备的丝缕玉衣。

☆玉衣又称"玉匣"，在汉代，是帝王和高级贵族死时穿的殓服。以玉衣作殓装的制度，可上溯到东周时代的"缀玉面罩"和缀玉片的衣服。

☆"秦汉南疆"南越国历史专题陈列，通过展示两广地区具有代表性的秦汉时期考古发现，概述岭南地区的区域面貌、族群构成及基本的社会发展状况，展现了岭南地区逐步发展并最终融入统一多民族国家的历史进程。重点文物有铜蒜头壶、"张仪"铜戈、"蕃禺"汉式铜鼎等。

☆"蕃禺"汉式铜鼎出土于南越文王墓，铜鼎蹄足矮胖，面有棱线。"蕃禺"即番禺，为秦时南海郡治，后为南越国都。这件铜鼎说明广州建城至少已有2200多年的历史了，是广州城市建设史的重要物证。

☆ "张仪"铜戈出土于南越文王墓，铜戈内上铭刻"王四年相邦（张）义"等十九字。"王四年"即秦惠文王后元四年（前321年）；"义"通"仪"，说明该铜戈可能为秦相张仪所督造。据推测，铜戈应由平定岭南的秦国将士带来，是秦统一岭南的重要历史物证。

☆杨永德伉俪捐赠藏枕专题陈列以香港知名鉴藏家和实业家杨永德伉俪捐赠的200余件瓷枕为主要展出内容。瓷枕的烧制始于隋唐时期，在宋元时期最为繁荣。瓷枕既是中国古代常见的日用器具，又蕴含丰富文化元素，不仅反映出胎釉、烧制等工艺技法，而且体现了审美与实用的和谐统一，在古代陶瓷艺术中占有独特地位。

☆南越木简2004年底于南越国宫署遗址出土，整简和残简共一百多枚，总字数超过一千，均为木质。字体多为隶书，也有篆书。简文为南越王宫的文书档案，包括管理、财务、军事、法律等内容，涉及纪年、地名、职官、宫室管理、物品进贡、奖罚制度、社会风俗等方面，为研究秦汉史，尤其是南越国历史提供了第一手文字资料，填补了岭南地区简牍考古的空白，堪称"岭南第一简"。

☆杏形金叶出土时覆盖在丝缕玉衣的面罩上，金片共八片，形状、纹饰相同。主题纹样为二尖角对羊纹。金片上下左右各有小孔一对，用以缝缀丝线。同类型的羊纹金饰片在河北、江苏、山东等地的汉墓中也有出现。在金属上刻动物图像多为北方草原文化的风格，羊纹金饰片的传播反映了各地文化的交流与融合。

广州市南越王博物院（王墓展区）

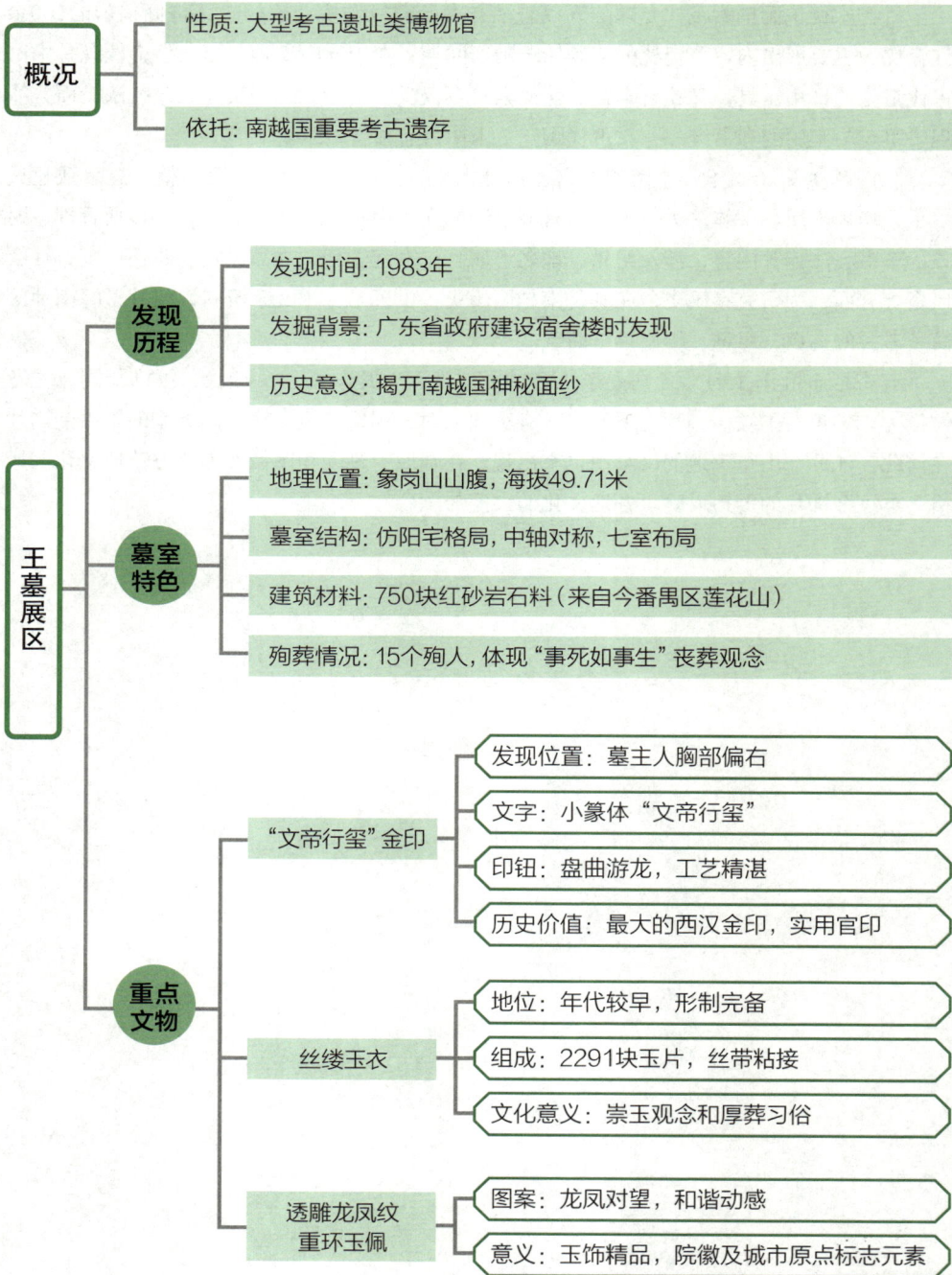

概况
- 性质: 大型考古遗址类博物馆
- 依托: 南越国重要考古遗存

王墓展区

发现历程
- 发现时间: 1983年
- 发掘背景: 广东省政府建设宿舍楼时发现
- 历史意义: 揭开南越国神秘面纱

墓室特色
- 地理位置: 象岗山山腹，海拔49.71米
- 墓室结构: 仿阳宅格局，中轴对称，七室布局
- 建筑材料: 750块红砂岩石料（来自今番禺区莲花山）
- 殉葬情况: 15个殉人，体现"事死如事生"丧葬观念

重点文物

"文帝行玺"金印
- 发现位置: 墓主人胸部偏右
- 文字: 小篆体"文帝行玺"
- 印钮: 盘曲游龙，工艺精湛
- 历史价值: 最大的西汉金印，实用官印

丝缕玉衣
- 地位: 年代较早，形制完备
- 组成: 2291块玉片，丝带粘接
- 文化意义: 崇玉观念和厚葬习俗

透雕龙凤纹重环玉佩
- 图案: 龙凤对望，和谐动感
- 意义: 玉饰精品，院徽及城市原点标志元素

第十五节　广州市陈家祠

一、讲解要点

（一）概述

1.陈家祠的地理位置和功能。

2.陈家祠的美誉和地位。

3.陈家祠的朝向和整体布局。

（二）陈家祠的装饰艺术

1.陶塑瓦脊的数量、产地、工艺、题材、寓意。

2.灰塑的位置、长度、工艺、特点。

3.砖雕的位置、材料、工艺、特点。

4.首进院落的彩绘门神、木雕屏门。

5.中进聚贤堂的石雕月台、用途。

6.后进祖堂的用途。

二、中文讲解词示例

【欢迎词】

游客朋友们，大家好！欢迎来到陈家祠参观游览。

【概述】

陈家祠又名陈氏书院，位于广州市中山七路，于清光绪十四年（1888年）开工建设，光绪十九年（1893年）落成。是广东省各县陈氏宗族合资捐建的"合族祠"，是为参与捐资的陈氏宗族子弟到广州城备考科举、候任、交纳赋税、办理诉讼等事务而提供的临时居所。1959年这里被政府辟为广东民间工艺馆，1988年被国务院列为全国重点文物保护单位。2002年和2011年以"古祠留芳"入选"羊城八景"。陈家祠为何被誉为"岭南建筑艺术明珠"呢？因为这里集广东民间建筑装饰艺术之大成，在建筑构件上巧妙地运用木雕、砖雕、石雕、灰塑、陶塑、铜铁铸和彩绘等装饰工艺，是一座传统建筑装饰艺术的璀璨殿堂，也是广东现存规模最大、保存完好、装饰精美的祠堂式建筑。*速记 三雕（木、石、砖）、二塑（陶、灰）、一铸（铜铁）、一画（彩绘壁画）。

陈家祠坐北朝南，主体建筑面宽和纵深都是80米，平面呈正方形，布局为三路三进，由9座厅堂、6个院落、10座厢房和青云巷组成，主体建筑面积6400平方米。*速记 九堂六院。*技巧 可展示陈家祠主体建筑平面图，从外到内、从高到低讲解。

【陶塑】

请大家向上看，陈家祠的脊饰主要有陶塑和灰塑，这是岭南地区所独有的建筑装饰艺术。

屋顶最高处是陶塑瓦脊，陈家祠一共有11条陶塑瓦脊。陶塑瓦脊在广东佛山石湾制作，分段烧制，烧成温度高达1230摄氏度。制成后运到建筑屋脊上进行组装。为了减轻对建筑的压力，瓦脊往往是空心设计。而在施釉方面，因为岭南地区阳光比较强烈，为了避免反光对观赏的影响，瓦脊一般都会选择较为暗沉的釉色。陶塑题材以粤剧故事和本地民间传说为主，由于人物最多，也被称为"公仔脊"。大家看到屋脊最上方的左右两侧各有一只龙头鱼尾的动物，这就是鳌鱼。为什么鳌鱼上了屋顶呢？传说中鳌是龙的九子之一，它喜欢吞火还爱吐水，所以古人将它放置在屋顶，希望它像个"消防员"一样能起到防火消灾的作用。同时，也有对本族参加科举考试的人能考取功名、独占鳌头的期盼。*技巧 使用"问答法"可活跃气氛，促进游客和导游间的交流互动。

【灰塑】

在陶塑瓦脊的下方，色彩较为鲜艳的脊饰则运用了灰塑工艺。灰塑主要分布在陈家祠厅堂的正脊上，作为陶塑脊饰的基座，垂脊、连廊、山墙、廊、门窗、檐等位置也有灰塑装饰，总长度达2562米。灰塑在民间被称为"灰批"，工匠们首先用竹钉、铁钉、铜丝或铁丝、瓦片等搭建骨架，然后在石灰中加入稻草、糯米、红糖、草纸等材料进行发酵。用发酵后的膏状物先在骨架上塑形，等干燥后再给成型的灰塑上色，就完成了所有工序。灰塑的所有制作都必须在现场完成，不能预制组装。灰塑密实坚硬，防水性较好，很适合作为建筑装饰材料。由于广州气候炎热多雨，灰塑比较容易褪色，因此陈家祠每隔6到7年就会对灰塑进行一次保养。

【砖雕】

在正门两侧的青砖外墙上，有六幅大型砖雕。广东砖雕多选用东莞精炼烧制的水磨青砖为材料，在雕刻之前，砖雕艺人根据图案内容安排层次，做好规划布局，并将每一块青砖详细勾画标记；然后采用多种技法雕出所属部分的纹样；最后把砖块依次镶嵌在墙上。为什么广东砖雕有"挂线砖雕"之称呢？因为砖与砖之间的接缝细如丝线，整齐连贯。砖雕画面层次较多、立体感强，人物鸟兽形态传神生动、立体逼真。*技巧 七绝工艺可各选取一处详细解说。

【首进院落】

进入大门后请大家回头看看这两扇高5.6米的大门，门上有一对4米高的彩绘门神。红脸的是秦琼，黑脸的是尉迟恭，这两位将军的画像绘在门上，据说可以守家护院，辟邪保平安。

现在我们身处陈家祠的首进门堂，是迎送宾客的地方。转身可见四扇双面镂空木雕大屏门，既阻隔视线又能分割空间，上部镂空部分有利于院内通风透气。这扇屏门在贵宾来临或祭祖大典时会全部打开，以表达对来宾的尊重。

现在请大家跟随我来到屏门后面，我们现在看到正中屏门下边的两块裙板。这幅木雕作品的主体雕刻了老竹盘曲的形象，构成了一个"福"字。而"竹"又与"祝"谐音，因此有"祝福"之意。我们再将这个"福"字拆开，左半部分像草书的"多"字，右半部分像草书的"寿"字，又表达出"多福多寿"的寓意。而这幅图的题字为"青春发达大器晚成"。意思是说：期望年轻一辈，像这竹子上的嫩芽一样，青春有为，蓬勃生长；而若是科举不中，也不要气馁，要继续努力，迟早会老竹吐嫩芽，大器晚成。

【中进聚贤堂】

各位游客朋友，现在我们登上石雕月台，这里的栏杆望柱头雕有一盘盘菠萝、杨桃、桃子、佛手等岭南佳果，既富有岭南风情，又寄寓了陈氏子孙终年以果品祭祀天地神灵和祖先，祈求保佑的心意。聚贤堂位于陈家祠的中心，是陈家祠最大的厅堂，也是当年陈氏族人议事聚会的地方。

【后进祖堂】

现在我们从青云巷来到陈家祠后进祖堂，这里是供奉祖先牌位的地方，在祖堂有五座大型的木质神龛。最多的时候，陈家祠供奉了多达1.2万个祖先牌位。每年春秋两季，陈姓族人在此举行隆重的合族祭祖仪式，以示对祖先的虔诚敬意。

【结束语】

郭沫若曾经赋诗称赞陈家祠："天工人可代，人工天不如。果然造世界，胜读十年书。"希望大家通过今天的参观，能感受到陈家祠这颗"岭南建筑艺术明珠"的魅力。我的讲解到此结束，谢谢大家的聆听！

三、英文讲解词示例

Chen Clan Ancestral Hall in Guangzhou

Hello everyone, welcome to the Chen Clan Ancestral Hall! I am your tour guide.

The Chen Clan Ancestral Hall, also known as Chen Clan Academy, is located in No.7 Zhongshan Road, Guangzhou. The construction started in 1888 and was completed in 1893 during the reign of Emperor Guangxu in the Qing Dynasty. It is a family shrine donated by the Chen clan in various counties of Guangdong Province, serving as a temporary residence for the Chen clan donors' juniors when they prepared for the imperial examination in Guangzhou.

In 1959, it was explored to house the Guangdong Folk Art Museum by the government. In 1988, it was listed as a Major Historical and Cultural Site Protected at the National Level by the State Council. In 2002 and 2011, it was selected as one of the "Eight Sights of Guangzhou" known as "Gu Ci Liu Fang" which means ancestral hall with a high reputation. Why is the Chen Clan Ancestral Hall recognized as the "Pearl of Lingnan Architectural Art"? Because it is a splendid epitome of Cantonese traditional folk decorative arts, and it shows skillful use of wood carving, brick carving, stone carving, plaster sculpture, pottery sculpture, copper and iron casting, and color painting. **Moreover,** it is the largest, preserved and fine-decorated ancestral hall in Guangdong.

The front gate of the Chen Clan Ancestral Hall faces south. **Covering an area of 6,400 square meters, the whole architecture is in square formation,** 80 meters on each of its four sides. **The layout consists of** 3 passages and 3 entries. **There are 9 halls, 6 courtyards, 10 side rooms and Qingyun Lane.**

Please look up. The roof ridge decorations of the Chen Clan Ancestral Hall mainly include pottery sculpture and plaster sculpture, which are unique architectural decorative arts in Lingnan area.

The top roof ridges are decorated with pottery sculptures. There are 11 such main roof ridges in the Chen Clan Ancestral Hall. The pottery sculptures were made in Shiwan, Foshan, Guangdong Province. They were fired in separate kilns at a temperature of 1230℃ before they were set on the roofs of the building. In order to reduce the pressure on buildings, the pottery sculptures are often hollow in design. **Because of the strong sunlight in Lingnan area, to** minimize the impact of light reflection from the pottery sculptures, **they were generally glazed in a dusky color. The pottery sculptures have themes taken from Cantonese opera stories and local folklores, and are known as** "Figure Ridges", **for there are** many human figures **in them. We can see a creature with a dragon head and a fish tail on the two ends of a roof ridge. This is Aoyu, an imaginary fish in ancient Chinese mythology.** Why is Aoyu placed on the roof ridge? **Story has it that Aoyu is one of the nine sons of the Chinese dragon. It likes to swallow fire and spray water, so the ancients put it there, hoping that it could** prevent fire and wipe out ill fortunes like a firefighter. **In addition, there were also expectations that the Chen clan members who took the imperial examinations could** take lead and succeeded like the soaring dragon.

The bright ridge decoration under pottery roof ridge is made of plaster sculptures, serving as the base for pottery sculptures. They are mainly used on the roof ridges of the main halls and rooms. The total length of the plaster sculptures in the Chen Clan Ancestral Hall is 2562 meters. Plaster sculpture is called "batch putty sculpture" among the folks. **The craftsmen first build its skeleton with** bamboo nails, iron nails, copper wires or iron wires, tiles. **Then add** straw, glutinous rice, brown sugar, straw paper **and other materials for** fermentation. **The fermented paste is first** molded **on the skeleton, and then dried and** colored. **The entire production of plaster sculpture** must be completed on site instead of prefabricated. **The plaster sculpture is dense, hard and waterproof. So it is an ideal building decoration material. Because the** plaster sculptures are easy to fade due to the hot and rainy climate **in Guangzhou, the Chen Clan Ancestral Hall have to maintain them** every 6-7 years.

There are six large brick carvings on the blue brick peripteral walls on both sides of the main entrance. Guangdong brick carvings mostly use terrazzo-like blue bricks refined and fired in Dongguan as materials. Before carving, the craftsman first plans the layout according to the pattern, and outlines the marks of each grey brick in detail, then uses various techniques to carve the patterns, and finally embeds them on the wall one by one. Why is Guangdong brick carving known as "brick carving of hanging lines"? Because the seams between bricks are as thin as silk thread and consistent. Because there are many layers when carving figures creating the 3D impression, the figures on the brick are vivid and lifelike.

After entering the gate, please look back at these two 5.6-meter-high gates with a pair of 4-meter-high painted door gods. The one with a red face is Qin Qiong, and the other with a black face is YuChi Gong. It is said that painting the portraits of these two generals on the door can have them guard the house, ward off evil spirits and keep peace.

Now we are at the first entrance hall of the Chen Clan Ancestral Hall. It is the place to welcome and see off guests. When you turn around, you can see four large screen doors with hollowed-out wood carvings. They can ensure privacy and provide separate space, and the hollowed-out part on the upper part is good for ventilation across the courtyard. This screen is opened completely when distinguished guests visit the Hall or during the ancestor worship to show respect for the guests.

Now please follow me to the backside of the screen doors. What we are looking at right now is two apron boards right below the central screen doors. This woodcarving work presented the image of the curved old bamboo. Forming the shape of the Chinese character "Fu" which means "blessing." Also "bamboo" shares the same Chinese sound as "wish", so the work means "wish you well". Besides, the left part of the Chinese character "Fu" looks like the Chinese character "Duo" which means "many", and the right part looks like "Shou" which means "longevity". The inscription on this picture is "Young minds bloom lively, great minds mature slowly." It reflects the hope that younger generation would thrive vigorously like the buds on this bamboo. For those who failed in the imperial examinations, the inscription also encouraged them to keep working hard.

Now let's get on the stone carving platform. The fence here is carved with the patterns of plates of Lingnan fruits such as pineapples, carambolas, peaches and bergamots, which showcases Lingnan customs and embodies the thoughts of Chen's descendants for blessing. The Gathering Hall Juxian Tang is the largest hall in the center here for the Chen people to hold the consultative meetings.

Now we come to the Rear Hall dedicated to ancestor worship, where the ancestral tablets are enshrined. There are five large wooden shrines in this Hall. At its peak, the Chen Clan

Ancestral Hall enshrined as many as 12,000 ancestral tablets. Every spring and autumn, the people surnamed Chen hold a grand family ancestor worship ceremony here to show their sincere respect for their ancestors.

A famous poet Guo Moruo once wrote a poem praising the Hall: "The natural endowment can be achieved by human, but the fine craftsmanship can never be well-replaced by heaven. To build a marvelous world is better than reading for ten years." Hope today's tour has left you great impression about our Pearl of Lingnan Architectural Art—the Chen Clan Ancestral Hall. Here I will conclude our tour. Thank you for your time!

四、综合知识

☆1988年，陈家祠被国务院列为全国重点文物保护单位，2002年和2011年以"古祠留芳"入选"羊城八景"，2008年被评为国家4A级旅游景区，2017年被评为国家一级博物馆，被誉为"广州文化名片"。

☆陈家祠集中了广东民间建筑装饰艺术之大成，被誉为"岭南建筑艺术明珠"，与佛山祖庙、肇庆悦城龙母祖庙并称为"岭南古建筑三瑰宝"。

☆陈家祠1959年被政府辟为广东民间工艺馆，1994年更名为广东民间工艺博物馆，是收藏以广东为主兼及全国的民间工艺精品的艺术类博物馆。目前馆藏已达2万多件，其中有近3000件（套）属于国家级珍贵文物。牙雕、榄雕、岭南押花、广彩、手工打金、石湾陶塑、广州玉雕等工艺定期在陈家祠进行展演。

☆陈家祠在建筑构件上巧妙地运用木雕、砖雕、石雕、灰塑、陶塑、铜铁铸和彩绘等装饰艺术，这"三雕、二塑、一铸、一画"，又称"岭南七绝"。

☆清代，只有宗族中有人获取高官和功名，祠堂门前才可设置石鼓，石鼓越大象征着地位越高。在陈家祠动工两年后，族人陈伯陶被钦点为探花郎，清政府特许陈氏家族在宗祠前设立巨型石鼓，以示表彰。

☆跟岭南其他祠堂的石鼓比起来，陈家祠大门两侧的石鼓特别大，连座高2.55米，直径达1.4米，是目前广东省现存规模最大的石鼓，也是陈家祠门第与功名的象征。石鼓精雕细琢，饰有日月神、八仙和多子多福等题材的高浮雕图案。

☆大门前东侧石鼓基座，雕有"日神"，象征阳刚和男性；西侧石鼓基座，雕有"月神"，象征阴柔和女性。他们手拿阴阳镜、照妖镜，寓意"驱除邪恶"。日月神是我国原始社会自然崇拜的对象，也代表了古人对天地和日月星辰等自然属性的敬畏。

☆陈家祠正门高达5.6米，宽4.1米，大门板上的两尊彩绘门神像各高4米，运用工笔重彩技法描绘。其中红脸的是秦琼，黑脸的是尉迟恭。

☆跨进大门进入首进正厅，迎面看到的是四扇镂空双面雕屏风。每扇屏风高4.5米，宽1.3米，上面镂雕"渔樵耕读""渔舟唱晚""衣锦还乡"等以传统题材为主的画面，构思精巧，雕工精细。

☆东西厢房为陈氏弟子的读书处，东厢房壁画绘《滕王阁图》，西厢房绘《夜宴桃李》，以文人雅士为题材，恰好与厢房的书房功能相匹配。

☆聚贤堂有20扇雕花门档，堪称"木刻钢刀雕就的历史故事长廊"。东厅四扇为《三国演义》故事，有"长坂坡救阿斗""赤壁之战""三顾茅庐""三英战吕布"；中间门档雕刻的内容为从商周到宋代的历史故事、民间传说等，如《隋唐演义》中的"太白退番书"，《说唐全传》中的"郭子仪上寿""薛仁贵东征"等；西厅四扇为《水浒传》中的"拳打镇关西""血溅鸳鸯楼""三打祝家庄"等内容。

☆陈家祠的陶塑瓦脊共计11条，在广东佛山石湾制作，是广东现存最大型、最华丽的清代传统建筑装饰。脊饰以龙凤、瑞兽、山水、花鸟为饰，又以粤剧传统剧目的历史故事、民间传说为题材塑造的相关场景为主。在11条陶塑瓦脊中，以聚贤堂的规模最为宏大。整条瓦脊共塑有224个人物，如同一个巨大的舞台，生动而直观地讲述着一个个传奇故事。

☆陈家祠的灰塑规模宏大，内容丰富，技艺精湛，造型灵活多变，动物、花卉、山水、人物全部可以凸出墙体，呈现立体的画面。最具代表性的是山墙垂脊上的十二对灰塑狮子，体型巨大，全身朱红色，张口突眼，神态各异，蹲伏在垂脊上，表现出一副护卫的姿态。这些灰塑狮子代表了广东灰塑工艺的最高水平。

☆蝙蝠也是陈家祠的灰塑装饰艺术中运用较多的动物。蝙蝠的"蝠"与"福"谐音，象征福寿、福气、幸福等，是民间最受喜爱的吉祥物之一。陈家祠的灰塑蝙蝠造型夸张，和蔼可亲，生动美观，寓意吉祥。如：蝙蝠前面有一串铜钱，称"福在眼前"；两只蝙蝠叠在一起，称"福上加福"；五只蝙蝠围绕"寿"字，称"五福捧寿"；蝙蝠口中含着如意绳结、桃子，称"福寿如意""福寿双全"……故有"卢沟桥的狮子数不清，陈家祠的福字数不完"一说。

☆陈家祠的铁铸装饰主要用在中进聚贤堂前的月台上。聚贤堂前月台的铁铸通花栏板以精美通透、色泽灰黑的铁铸镶嵌在石雕构件之中，与周围浅白的石栏杆形成鲜明的对比，装饰效果十分突出，铁铸内容有"麒麟凤凰送玉书""三羊启泰""金玉满堂"等。

☆陈家祠的石雕多采用花岗石制成。花岗石耐腐、耐风化，是岭南建筑的常用材料。石雕的装饰题材十分丰富，并具有一定含义，如牡丹象征富贵，菊花象征高雅，龙、凤、麒麟象征吉庆祥和，鹿、鹤寓意长寿，等等。

广州市陈家祠

概况
- 位置: 广州市中山七路
- 建设时间: 清光绪十四年 (1888年) 至清光绪二十年 (1894年)
- 功能: 陈氏宗族子弟来广州备考科举、办事的临时居所
- 现状: 广东民间工艺博物馆、全国重点文物保护单位、"羊城八景"之一
- 誉称: 岭南建筑艺术明珠

建筑特色
- 布局: 三路三进, 正方形
- 装饰艺术: 木雕、砖雕、石雕、灰塑、陶塑、铜铁铸、彩绘

大门外
- **陶塑瓦脊**
  - 数量: 11条
  - 特点: 人物为主 (公仔脊), 鳌鱼寓意防火消灾、独占鳌头
  - 制作: 佛山石湾, 分段烧制, 空心设计
- **灰塑**
  - 分布: 正脊、垂脊、连廊、山墙等
  - 特点: 现场制作, 防水性好, 需定期保养
  - 制作: 搭建骨架, 塑形, 上色
- **砖雕**
  - 数量: 6幅
  - 材料: 东莞水磨青砖
  - 特点: 挂线砖雕, 层次丰富, 形态生动
  - 制作: 规划布局, 雕刻纹样, 镶嵌墙上